BULLY

The Life and Crimes of a Chelsea
HEAD-HUNTER

MARTIN KING
AND
GAETANO BUGLIONI

HEAD-HUNTER BOOKS

FIRST PUBLISHED IN DECEMBER 2006
BY HEAD-HUNTER BOOKS

Copyright © 2006 Martin King and Gaetano Buglioni
Photographs copyright © Gaetano Buglioni and Martin King

ISBN 0-9548542-9-2

HEAD-HUNTER BOOKS

Printed in Great Britain

Contents

CONTENTS

Acknowledgements

Alex Parker, Hicky, Babs, Greenaway – RIP, Eccles, Colin Daniels, Tony C, Mark Cator, Martin King, Dave Ayling, Rol, Dave Gray, Big Andy, Lee Proctor, Kingsley, Chris from Kilburn, Scotty Tauton, Billy Matthews, Dessie F, Bugsy, Jerry Kilburn, Dave and Ian Sim, Vincent Drake, Giles, Beast, Cooper, Holte, Pat Dolan, Kevin, Chris, Reigate, Prykey, T. Walker, John Carlin, Geordie, Tim, Martin D, Beastly, The Montys, Nigel and Phil, John and Billy Bud, Terry Smith, Jason Mariner, Dave Scotcher, Skinhead John, Skinhead Paul, Panther, Bob the tee shirt, Big Pete, P.J., Stuart Glass, Delboy, Steve Parker, Sky Mattie, Gary Germaine, Freddie, Windmill, Wingnut, Terry Kent, Lee D, Jason, Barry Ewings, James, Darren, Micky Elliott, Tommy White, Ben, Dave, Lee, Gerry, Ian and Dave Lewisham, Jimmy, Tony Canning Town, Nic, Paul, Ray Winstone, Ronnie Fox, Ronnie Austin, Herby Dave, Ray, Peter and the rest of the family. The Adams, Tommy, Terry, Patrick and Danny. Peter and Nollie, Lawrence

Cheeseman, Andy Howard, Stuart, Stuart Taylor, Jock, Micky Hayes, Charlie, Kelly Alf, John Rambo, Jason Edwards, Danny Miller, Denton, Dave Smith, Paul Dorrey, John Lyden, Jimmy Lyden and family, Leggsy, Micky Nagle, The Graneys, Brendon Smyth, Carol Smyth, Chalky, Paul Cook, Slighty, Perry Fenwick, Bingle, Gerry Smith, Irish Colin, Barry Fields, Mark Murray, Geordie Colin, Logs, Dave Cronin, Jock and Lesley, Kathy C.F.C., Lisa, Tina, Nicki, Marion, Easha, Lizzie, Hanna, Angie, Barry, Charlene, Stevie Woods, Bob and sons, Kevin Avis, Paul H, Selina, Kelly, Cindy, Adrian, John, Dave and Jimmy, Mark Stamos, Deach, Brendon Mc, The Flanagans, Tony Murphy, Lenny Compton, The Buglioni Family, John Powell, Mark and Julie Vicars, Booster, Danny, Janine and Scott, Steff, Billy Rice, Sam, Elliot, Craig Wynn, Savva, Ben Craig, Kelly, John, Rudi and Luke, Paul Ginotti, Peter Henshaw, Richard Smith, Paul Hutley, Stuart Livermore, Richard Harris, Paul Hazel, Tom, Lee, Pike, Battersea Bill, Nigel, Chrissie, Chris H, Mick Nichols, Big Colin, Worzzel, Tom, George The Greek, Tony White, Mr. C, Corkie, Spencer Clarke, Dermot, Tully, Lol Hardy (Top Tattooist), Vidos, Mark Willis, Maxine, Melody, Lesley, Billy, Terry Battersea, Terry Hopkinson, Richard Squash, Perry AFC, Connie, Debbie, Pam, Paul T, Dave Johnny and Chrissie Avis, Lee Bowler, Tiger AFC, Viczeroy Gaines, Colin Waldron, Nigel Hope, Robert Robertson, Chrissie Weight, Paul Smith, Hugo Boss, Tunde, Gary Dixon, Dave W, Barry Wolsey, Bins and Lou, Tee, Clinton Brown, Bins No 2, Fodge, S, B, Jackie Manning, Debbie Jackson, Janice Blyth, Brenda Parker, Jeff Day, Terry and Brian Robertson, Terry Hoffman, Stephen Price, Hubert Howard, Gra, Jade and Janine, Carlo, Kyppa, Kenny Stapleton, Colin Dunne, Colin Lake, Auldrey, Tony and Pat Bones, Muswell Hill Ricky and Tony, Ronald the German, Skitzy, Barrels, Big Robbie, Rossi, Kieron, Bugsey Mile End, Roy Collins, Porky, Roy Parker, Harold and Gerald Harris, Steve Dent, Big Russell and Son, Jeff Tierney, Debbie Radley, Peter Haddington, John Sooter, Terry

Knight, Big Grant, Louisa Mansfield, Sebastian Mansfield and Herman, Lil, Steve Tombs, Bernadette, Denise, Sonia, Alan Unswick, Todd Carty, Mick Mahoney, Jamie Woodcock, Lil Bill, John, Keith, Higginbottom, Paul, Philpot, Glen Alappisela, Phil Daniels, Ritchie Kippa (Highway), Micky Qleary, Colin and Esta, Darrio, Luigi and all the Napoli bosses and Napoli's big boss and all in Curva A! Richard Sheilds, Tracey Weaver, Lesley Lincoln, Chris and Rita Falco, Matt, Johnson (W.H.U.) Jamie Foreman, Terry Marsh, Bradley Walsh, Jeff Pyke, Paul B, Dave Patents, Charlie Creed, Mills, Paul Williams, (Reggie), Mensie, (Angelic Upstarts), Barnet Mark, 12 Bar Girls, Tinzel and band, Stretch, Manni, Scouse Jim, Scouse Darren, Adolf, Raymond Clarke, Kim Priest, Susan Cowup, Alan Grimble, Mazda, Tony Howard, Warren Glass, Goodchild, Simon Jones, Jock McDonald, Karen and Sarah, (Bananarama) Nigel and wife, Gary Kelly, Tony Britten, Tony London, Steve Barker, Brian Harrison, Gary Alliard, Donna, Simon Robinson, Ossie, Zac, Noel Gallagher, David Lee Smith, Cardiff's firm in Enfield, Roy, Ginger Bob, Jimmy Morris, Richard Driscoll, John Kidd, Francesco (Napoli), Matti Robson, Kortney, Rory (Johnny Boy) King, Mandy King, Posh and Barney. Barney, Danny and Joe Millington, Chalky, Mark Phillips, Paul Creasy, Lee, Bernie Walker, Michael Hughes, Leftari, Dave Chinnery, Little Tony, Clinker, Arnie, Gary Boulter, Steve Mose, Nimsy, Anthony Thomson, Neal N.S., Dave Wilson, Micky Q, Rooster, Mortz, Phil and Lesley, Dave Sporoni, Paul Harvey, Kelly and Neil, A.D., Tommy, Doo Daa, Sue Roach, Irish Tom, Linda, Ashley, Keely, Sweeney, Steve Dawes, Nicky Compton, Frank the Golden Boy, Pete, Dene, Boo, Steve Norris, Corky, Ben and Michael from The Roby, Martin Buglioni, Maurice and Clare, Mandy King, White Horse FC, Big John, Little Debbie, Melody Hilliard Jones, Sylvia Gate, Berger Road School, and Upton House, Mr. Slack, Carol Graves, Pat Vincent, Pat Bow, Pauline Street, Scrag x Kenny Giles, Chris Weight, Peter Lyons, Peter O'Leary, Alex Lawson, Michael Dent, Valerie, Tony

Pitchfork, Bonnie Lee, John Sciterio, Louisa, Simon Robinson, Debbie, Terry Batten, Terry Hoppinson, Gail, Tracey Weaver, Graham Finnegan, Barry Simmonds, Debbie Grania, Caroline, Donna, Denise, Dave J at the CFC stool, Claire Jepson GP, Steve Jones, John Dougley, Frank Shaw, Bernie, Martin King (Queens) Lorraine, Zetty and Kas, Lal, Mandy, Chris and Rita, John Kidd and Billie, Irene Brown, Rossana, Lindsey, Janet Davey, Sharon Jackson, H and Liza, Annette, Penny, Abbi, Michael Skins, Eddie Carpenter, Judge Jules, Ange and Colette, Blieu, Barry, Stephen, Michael, Daniel, Tom, Brian, Harry, Ryan, Rob, Mark, Tony, Olly, Craig, Johnstone, Ben, Liam, James, Froudy, Richie, Birdie, Nick, Darren, Joson, Fisher, Ciaran, Ginger Tom, Fleming, Serena, Steve, Chris, Dave, The Graneys, Steve, Sasha, Paris, Georgina, Louie, Yazz, Little One. A big thank you to Ross at 'Photo Perfect' in Enfield Town. The Napoli Testi Matti Fabio, Angelo, Daniele, Enzo, Marco, Salvatore, Ernesto, Genni, Angioletto.

I'd like to dedicate this book to my
Ma and Pa and my Godfather, Tom Hill.
Thanks for everything

Love to my special girls, Victoria and Alexandra Buglioni
My two princesses xxx

My Godchildren Liam Nagle and Jamie Winstone xx

Love and Best Wishes to everyone in this book x

"It don't stop, it never ends."

Gaetano Buglioni

INTRODUCTION
by
Ray Winstone

I was born in the East End of London in Hackney Hospital and grew up in Bethnal Green. As a kid, it was very different to how it is now. The place had a completely different buzz to it. It all kind of changed after the Myra Hindley case. Before that, us kids were allowed to roam and play out in the streets and have fun. There's that old cliché that you could leave your front door open, and that was very true. People used to leave their front door keys dangling on a bit of string behind the letterbox. In them days, you knew who your neighbours were and you knew they were the same as you. Then people's homes were demolished, high-rise flats were built, and that broke the community spirit. People were forced to live in these concrete rabbit hutches and no one knew who their neighbours were. Communities were destroyed as a result. Communities were divided and conquered and a way of life was changed forever.

As I grew older, I got into boxing and boxed for the Repton Club. I had 88 fights as an amateur. I started when I was about 13 and won the London N.A.B.C. finals 3 times and got to the National semis, but I broke a finger and couldn't appear in the final. I won the London area as a junior and then as a Class X and then as a senior.

I boxed up until I was 17 and then got into acting which, to be truthful, wasn't something that I'd always fancied doing? I used to go to the cinema every week with my dad and I was in a school play once. I knew in my heart I was never going to be a pro boxer and I suppose my mum and dad looked on the acting as a way of keeping me out of trouble, but then again I didn't really get in a lot of bother. You know how parents can be; perhaps they saw things before they happened? They're good at seeing things coming around corners.

I went to a drama school over in Hammersmith for a year and then I was asked to leave. The first thing I was in was 'Sunshine over Brixton' and then 'Scum.'

I met Bully when I was filming Robin of Sherwood in about 1983. In that was Michael Prade, Clive Mantle, Mark Ryan and Peter Williams. Even then, I didn't think I'd make it as an actor. I had a kind of different outlook on it. I saw it as a bit of a touch and felt privileged to be there. I saw myself different to a lot of actors. I learn my lines easy enough, no problems there. It's what I do, it's my game. Everyone's different but when I was a kid, I didn't read too well. I suppose I was lazy, but because I've had to read and learn my lines, my literacy skills improved.

Bully knew someone who was working on the 'Robin of Sherwood' set and him and me got talking and just hit it off straight away. We became good pals and used to go out and have a drink and a laugh together. One time we went down to Bristol, and went to a party on a boat, and got well hammered. At the time, he was living just off the Essex Road in North London and I was in Enfield so, as I say, we become good mates. Later on, we used to live around the corner to one another so we saw one another every day. We've always got on. He makes me laugh and he's always happy. I feel comfortable in his company. He wears his heart on his sleeve. I know all his family and he knows all of mine. I value him as a friend. I'm Godfather to his daughter, Victoria, and he's Godfather to one of my daughters.

I think him supporting Chelsea and being born in North London and bought up in East London is bollocks. He should be a fucking ashamed of himself. I suppose it could be worse; he could have supported Arsenal. We have a bit of banter between ourselves. I support West Ham so when we play each other I'll be on the phone giving it to him. I think he's frightened to come over to West Ham. The same when he got involved in all that shit out in Paris. I said to him "for fuck's sake Bully what are you playing at at your age?"

We've had a couple of poor results against Chelsea the last few seasons so I try to duck him when he calls me up. I can't say a lot but I think that's all about to change now we've got these two Argentinians. They look like blinding players. I don't want a team full of them and it would be nice to have a few home based players in the side, but once they settle in I think they'll come good. All these conspiracy theories surrounding their transfers to us make me laugh. The simple fact is Chelsea might not have had enough money to sign them.

I play in the West Ham celebrity team with Bradley Walsh, Todd Carty, Perry Fenwick and ex Hammer, Paul Brush. Bully's played about 30 times in goal for us and to tell you the truth he aint a bad keeper. I've also been to a few Chelsea games with him. I went to the Chelsea v Man City Full Members Cup Final at Wembley with Bully and I went to a night game against Leicester at Stamford Bridge, but West Ham's my team.

My dad was never really a big West Ham fan but he took me to all the England games in the 1966 World Cup finals, including the final against Germany. I don't know how he managed to get tickets for that; he must have pulled some strokes for that one. It's funny; I remember the whole game in black and white. It's been on the telly in colour but I remember the whole thing in black and white.

A couple of year's back I thought we'd lost me old mate Bully with his dodgy heart. I thought it was curtains for him. I was living and working out in America for a year and Vicky called me one night to say her dad was seriously ill, but he pulled through and he's right as rain now.

I don't see him so often now but we speak on the phone a lot. He's one nice fella, I think the world of him, and I love him to bits. He's a top bloke but I wished he supported his local football team.

Best Wishes,
Ray Winstone.

CHAPTER ONE

WILLY WONKA'S CHOCOLATE FACTORY

I was born in January 1957 in Islington, North London in Benwell Road, which is just off of the Holloway Road, which is just around the back of the old Arsenal football ground. I am one of three boys and the other two are Ralph and Clifford. My Grandad moved from Naples in Italy just after the Second World War. He moved over with his family. My mum was born in England but had Spanish parents. So as you can tell, I have a bit of Latin blood in me! All us boys were born at 93, Benwell Road because my parents, or more so my mum, didn't like the idea of giving birth at a hospital.

The house was a four-story town house and was rented and lived in by the whole of dad's family. We had one floor and my uncles, aunties, cousins and grandparents lived on the other floors. I can still remember them days, like playing out in the street with the rest of the kids in the neighborhood. That house would probably be worth about £5 million nowadays. We were a big family and were typical Italians. The men were very quick tempered and fiery and from what I can remember were in trouble most of the time.

My dad was an ashphalter and all my family did the same trade. An ashphalter, if you don't know, is someone that lays flat roofs. You use a big hot pot to melt the tar like substance, which is carried in metal buckets and tipped out to where you are working. Most of the tools used to spread the asphalt out flat are wooden. That's about the easiest way to describe the job. In the winter months, it's nice to get out of the chill by standing next to the boiling pot. There's an old wives tale that if you chew the black tar when it's still hard then it will clean your teeth and make then nice and white. The job is an art in itself. I think the trade was originally bought over here by the Italians. My granddad ran what was called "a bandit firm." They were called "bandit firms" because they broke away from the big companies that ran all the asphalting in those days. My granddad worked for himself and my dad worked with him. They went out and got all their own work and were one of the first firms to do it. There was a lot of Italian families in the area and my uncles were amongst the most respected. They never seemed to be far away from a bit of villainy. They were well known for it.

Islington in those days had its fair share of big crime families. There was the Austins, the Rileys, the Adams, the Flanagans, and us lot, the Buglioni's. My mum's family, the Palmers, were a big family but they weren't really into anything crooked. My dad was a very straight-laced man who would call a spade a spade, but he never really got in any bother, unlike one or two of my uncles. My Uncle Peter was well respected and by all accounts could have a fight. A few people have told me that at one time he was the governor. A lot of people were frightened of him and didn't like to get on the wrong side of him.

Just after I started school, we moved to a flat on the Gasgoigne Estate in Hackney, East London. It was lovely to have our own place as we left the rest of the relatives over in Islington, but I missed me mates and playing football in the street. I also missed seeing the crowds go past our road on their way to Highbury. On match days, we could hear the groans as the ball was stopped from going in the back of the net and we could hear the cheers and the jubilation as a goal was scored.

We used to play football in the playground of Shelburne School, which was my dad's old school, which was a big old fashioned Victorian school and the caretaker didn't mind us having a kick about in there.

The new flat over in Hackney was sheer luxury compared to what we'd left behind in Islington. We had a bathroom that we didn't have to share with anyone else and there were less arguments. Life was good. I could even see mum and dad were happier and at 7 years of age, I didn't have a care in the world. My dad was a nice man who was very strict with us but Mum used to let us get away with anything and she loved us boys. We'd get a kiss and a cuddle off of her but dad was different. He didn't really show his feelings and came across at times as a bit hard. We were poor but happy. In the old house, which my granddad had originally rented from the Housing Association, Circle 33, there was no electric lighting above the first floor. Whether the wiring was fucked or we couldn't afford light bulbs I don't know. We were kept in the dark like mushrooms a lot of the time. It's a wonder I didn't become a coalminer as I got older or ran away with the fair and worked on the ghost train! I was that used to the pitch black and the darkness. At Benwell Road we didn't even have proper beds. There was just mattresses laid on top of the threadbare carpet. I'll tell you it was rough. Our new place in Hackney was no palace and it wasn't a new development but it was a million times better than where we'd come from. We even had an inside toilet and an Ascot boiler that gave you hot water. There was no hot water at the old place and we used to bathe in a tin bath in the scullery where we used to have to boil kettles of water and top the tub up.

I went to school at Upton House in Hackney where I made loads of friends. One in particular I still see now. My Uncle Tom is married to my Auntie Rita who was a Buglioni. Well, Tom, is a rank Chelsea supporter and has been for years. All his family was Chelsea fans and Tom won us over with his tales of following The Blues. Tom was a West London boy and so his local team was Chelsea. Over in Hackney most of the kids supported either West Ham or Tottenham. There were a few Chelsea fans in the area but at our school there were only me and me mate Dave. Tom took me to my first game at Stamford Bridge, which was against Fulham and ended in a 1-1 draw. That was about 1967. Tom took me and my cousin, Ralph. I was so excited about going. No-one in my family had ever been interested in going to football. We used to live that close to Highbury but no-one from our lot would go to any of the games. At the Fulham game, we stood at the back of The Shed End, near the Bovril entrance. I suppose named after the tea bar that was at the back of the crumbling terraces. We were only small but standing up there, was a great view for us kids. I still have the programme for that game along with lots of others from them early years.

On the day of that game me dad dropped us off at Holloway Road tube station and from there it was down to Fulham Broadway by underground train. In them days Peter Osgood, Peter Houseman, Chopper Harris, Peter Bonetti and Co., were all just breaking into the first team. From that first day, I loved it, the crowds, the smell, and the noise. It was a day out which I've never forgotten. Tom made the day out for me and Ralph very special. He used to tell us all about the history of the club and the ground. He knew all about the players and the transfer gossip. He told us where to meet him if we got lost. He had it well organized. Tom's favourite player was Charlie Cooke and mine was Peter Bonnetti (The Cat). He just had that something about him. I went with Tom many times after that first game. That was money allowing. But in them days football was a working class sport and it was the entertainment of the masses. It was something like sixpence in old money for us kids to get in. Compare that to 50 pounds nowadays and that will give you some idea just how expensive football has become.

After a few seasons of standing at the back of the Shed end, we moved into the old West Stand and sat on the wooden benches, which were just below the main stand. You paid an extra couple of bob to transfer from The Shed into the benches but I was always drawn towards The Shed where all the dressers and singers would congregate. It was a compact sea of blue and white and the old rickety cover which covered about three quarters of the terracing width wise and about a third of the terracing depth wise, rocked from the atmosphere which was generated from that part of the ground. Heads would bob up and down as the mob jumped up and down as they sang 'Knees up Mother Brown'. I longed to get in the middle of the masses. Then one game I plucked up the courage and went off with a few mates right into the heart of The Shed. As I made my way through the crowds, ducking under the metal crash barriers, I looked back and gave Tom and Cousin Ralph a wave. After that, I traveled over to games with my mate, David Scotcher. By this time I was about 11 or 12. We were mates from school and still are to this day and I still see him over at Chelsea. We used to catch the train from Mile End to Fulham Broadway and we used to get chased every other week by West Ham fans. They cottoned on that me and Dave were Chelsea fans because a couple of times we came back on the tube a bit loud singing Chelsea songs and chanting. A few of the local West Ham boys, Panama and Buggsy, caught hold of us one weekend and chased us all over the place. They used to wait for us at the station, especially after night games. I think a West Ham boy on my estate had tipped them off as to the way we travelled back and forward to Chelsea. Basically we were grassed up. What ever happened to that good old East End code of practice?

When I got to about 13 years of age I started to hear certain names that were the leaders down at the Bridge. Greenwaway, Eccles, Premo, and Jesus were all names that would constantly crop up. These were the main players though I didn't know any of them personally. Tales of these blokes were legendary. How Greenaway had chased the Arsenal leader Johnny Hoy over Tower Bridge armed with a shotgun. How Eccles had led 200 of Chelsea's finest into the Park Lane at Tottenham and cleared it. These boys were the Generals. I remember a couple of visiting teams coming in the Shed in them days and trying to take it. One of them was Arsenal and the other West Ham. The West Ham game sticks in my mind because that was the first time I'd ever been chinned at football.

We got into the ground early and I presumed everyone that was packed under the cover of the Shed was Chelsea. In them days everyone used to get into the ground early. I remember looking around and seeing a few familiar faces. Kojack, a big, bald headed, black geezer, stood there with his muscley arms folded, but it was an eerie, strange atmosphere in there. Something wasn't quite right. The people around me looked edgy and nervous almost waiting and expecting something to happen. All of a sudden from nowhere there were West Ham fans everywhere, behind us, in front of us. They were everywhere. I was pushed from behind by Chelsea fans charging down the terraces at the West Ham mob. West hams mob stood firm and charged Chelsea back. I was caught in no mans land and I froze as fists bounced off my head. It seemed that I was frozen in time and things seemed to be happening in slow motion as I took one smack on the chin. I was out on my feet. My nose was pouring with blood as this big West Ham fan, about 30 years of age, cracked me again. They were men and we were young teenage boys. I was just a kid, like many of the boys that stood under the Shed. My eyes were streaming as the tears rolled down my cheeks. I was so embarrassed I didn't want the people around me to see me crying. Nowadays you wouldn't hit a young boy at football but in those days, West Ham and Millwall were grown men, and saw everyone as fair game. I can't say they were grown up men because they acted a bit retarded. I noticed a few blokes from my area in with the West Ham mob but the one pleasing thing was how Chelsea re-grouped and reclaimed The Shed, but the day was over for me as I made my way out of the ground even before a ball had been kicked. I was so upset and I suppose I was in shock. I had blood and sweat all over me and I was in a right old mess. That incident made me even more determined to get back for the next home game, but the next time I was to keep my guard up high, and get my punches in first.

Back at school in Hackney, I got a lot of stick off a few West ham fans but at the next game at Chelsea, a few lads came over, slapped me on the back, and asked me if I was all right. "You done well there kid" said one big skinhead as I poked my chest out. I felt a million dollars. At last, recognition!

The fashion in them days was Levi Sta Prest, Ben Sherman shirts and Dr. Martens. The majority of the Shed boys always looked smart. There was a few Herberts in there wearing white butchers' coats covered in graffiti with blue plastic star shaped pin on badges which had the players' photos on. Even at this early age I was into fashion and I was very conscious of how I looked. I'd bought my first pair of leather brogue shoes and a pair of two-tone mohair tonic trousers. I used to see someone dressed in something at football and thought, "that looks good." I'd go home and tell me mum and nine times out of ten she'd treat me. Sometimes though she wouldn't be that generous and one time she went off and got me a Cobb Castle shirt, which was a sort of cheap imitation Ben Sherman and what she done was, took the label out and tried to pass it off as a Ben Sherman. I never tumbled what she was up to until one day I was walking past a menswear shop at Victoria Park and I saw one of the shirts in the window. It was a cheap copy. I was gutted. I felt a fraud. I couldn't really complain because mum looked after us in other ways. There was always nice food on the table and she was a good cook. There was always bowls of pasta and salads and meatballs for us to tuck in to. We eat plentiful and healthily. My favorite was mum's spaghetti Bolognese. Granddad drank loads of red wine with his meals and I've taken after him. I just love red wine. It's my favourite tipple. I hear its good for you but not by the gallon which is how I drink it.

Arsenal was another firm that came in the Shed. That was about 1974 and the fashion then had changed slightly from Skinhead to Suedehead. The Suedehead look was Rupert the Bear, check trousers, loud flashy shirts and fringe and buckle loafers and the hair was grown and worn slightly longer.

Arsenal only took half of the Shed that day and the police removed them out of the ground twenty minutes before the end of the game. There was about 100 Arsenal in there and they were getting attacked by our boys from all sides. The Old Bill somehow managed to keep control although punches were thrown through the old bill ranks, by both sides. Arsenal were a mixture of young and old and they had a few black and Greek faces mixed in with them. Uncle Tom now knew that I was getting involved in bits of bother. Towards the end of that season, there was a night game down at The Bridge. For some reason or other, there was a pitch invasion and loads of us went onto the pitch and ran the length of the field to get to the away supporters. The police charged us back and to get away I climbed into the benches in the lower West Stand and standing there was me Uncle Tom who had witnessed first hand me leading the charge across the pitch. I don't think he was disgusted as he had a smile on his face but he did say, "what, are you doing?" I was caught bang to rights and after that I never ever went with Tom to football.

My first taste of following Chelsea away was at Birmingham and I travelled up there on one of the old football specials. I told my mum and dad I was going to watch Leyton Orient play but I sneaked off and watched Chelsea. The special was full right up and some bright spark in the mob thought it would be a good idea to go into the Birmingham Spion Kop End, which ran along the side of the pitch which was unusual because most teams home ends were behind one of the goals. In the end about 50 of us paid to get in there and almost immediately we were sussed out. It kicked off but we done well as we were under attack from all sides. The fighting went on all through the first half. In the end, we were being crushed up against the metal barriers. We were then forced, right down the front and I hate to admit it but a few faces slipped away. In the end there was only about 10 of us left and we got properly smashed. I was getting punched and kicked along the terraces and me and a couple of others ended up down near the corner flag next to where the bulk of the Chelsea fans were standing. The old bill done nothing but stood back and watched it. "Come on mate," I said to one copper, "it's like committing suicide."

"Well commit suicide then" was his straight-faced reply. In the end a barrage of coins and bricks forced us onto the pitch and by this time the old bill had seen enough and had had their bit of entertainment and threw us out of the ground. Five of us made our way back to New Street Station, bruised and bloodied. We waited for the rest of Chelsea to get back to the station and we then jumped on the special back to London.

Another game around this time was Brighton away in the 3rd round of the F.A.Cup. We won 2-0 and in that team was Peter Osgood who scored both goals, Gary Locke, Ron Harris, Steve Kember and Bill Garner. Inside the ground that day we went across the pitch before the game and cleared the Brighton end. I don't think there was even a punch thrown. We then beat Ipswich Town at home 2-0 in the 4th round with big Bill Garner getting both goals.

The 5th round saw us go to Sheffield Wednesday and fuck me did I get a hiding up there. We went into Wednesdays' massive big end behind the goal. The first train load to arrive in Sheffield got into their Kop no bother. It was a wide open terrace with, in them days, no cover on it. We stood at the back until we had everyone together and before we could get organized, we were attacked from all sides. The fighting was brutal and in the end, we were forced down to the bottom corner. As this was happening another trainload of Chelsea were trying to do the same thing as us but as soon as they were through the turnstiles then the Wednesday boys were waiting and forced them back. It was going off all over the place. I took a good few whacks that day. I was too game for me own good.

Around this time, I was planning to leave school or more to the fact, the school was hatching a plan to get rid of me and I couldn't wait. I'd known for a long time what I was going to be doing for a living and that was to follow my dad and my granddad and my uncles into asphalting. That was the only career for me. There was 1,500 boys in my school and I know you hear some people say they hated school but I can honestly say I didn't mind it. Hackney, where my school was, had everything and to me it was a great place to live. You had all the parks and commons, all the shops and the market, and the whole area was just alive and had a real good feel to it.

I used to go to the local youth club where we'd play reggae records and drink cheap cider. Janice Blyth was my first girlfriend and we met at the club and knocked about on the estate together. I suppose looking back it was a bit of a serious thing. I was 14, knocking on 15, so it was nice to have a bird. There was no sex involved and it was all innocent. I'd love to see her now just to have a chat about old times and really just to see what she looks like. She wasn't a bad old sort when she was younger. I'd love to meet up with all the old faces from them days. We used to have a disco at the club every couple of months and we'd dance to 'Skinhead Moonstomp' and 'Reggae in ya Jeggae. Liquidator' and all the old 'Tighten Up' stuff. The girls would dance in the middle of the dance floor and the boys would stand around the edge, backs to the wall sipping cups of luke warm cider. I was a seasoned drinker even in those days.

When I eventually left school I went to college and done a 5 year apprenticeship in asphalting. I done a day release and a block release from the firm I was working for. I also did my City and Guilds, which I passed with flying colours, which got me my qualifications to work as an asphalter. I was now a Spreader and it was hard at first because, like a lot of jobs, when you're training the money isn't that clever. There was kids that I knew who left school at the same time as I did and they were taking home 25 pounds a week working in a factory. My take home pay, as an apprentice was just £6 a week and a few of me mates took the piss out of me unmercifully. When I qualified, they were still on the same money, but mine went up and up and up. In those days asphalting was a good trade to get into. Nowadays there are so many new felts and coverings, that do the same, if not a better job, plus there are a few German systems on the market today that as made asphalting a bit of a dying trade. In the last 10 years, the trade as changed.

I worked hard but I still found time to play and watch football. I was never one for taking up boxing or Kung Fu or Karate. I never needed to as I had all my family around me who could more than look after themselves and me. The big thing on a Sunday afternoon was wrestling in the back garden over at our old house in Benwell Road. My uncles and cousins would all get into it and very often these contests would blow up into full scale punch ups.

It wasn't long before I started going to the Lyceum Ballroom and the Tottenham Royal. I had moved from Hackney to Edmonton in North London. We got an exchange through the council. I'd been getting in bits of bother on the estate and with gangs from Mile End and Limehouse. It all came to a head when I had a big gang looking for me when I came out of the local picture house one Saturday night. I think that was the final straw for mum and dad.

I fucking hated it in Edmonton although we had a 3 bedrooom flat. I just couldn't settle there. It was a new block of flats, which had won an award for its design and I think it got another award when they pulled them down. The place was crap, it was horrible. If you don't come from that area originally and you didn't go to school around there then the people were strange. I only stayed there a couple of years and kept myself to myself. The place was full of Tottenham fans who I hated. I lived on the Highmead Estate, which was just one block of flats with a green around it. My brothers moved back to live with the rest of the family over in Benwell Road and slowly the whole family, including uncles, aunties, cousins were drifting apart. There were times when we'd only come together at Christmas, New Year's Eve, weddings and funerals, which is not the best time or place to meet as Italian funerals can be very dramatic. You have the lot at Italian funerals. Mourning, drinking, eating, screaming, running up and down the road, and fighting. It's a bit like being at football. It's not an act; it's just in their personalities and in their upbringing. Italians are very emotional people. It can be a bit over the top at times. I witnessed some of these things at me granddad's and gran's funerals, not just with the oldens but I lost my cousin Tony when he was only 20 and that was so sad. We were a big family that had big funerals.

At 16 I moved back to Sebbon Street in Islington, just off of Upper Street. I got a council flat next door to the town hall. I put my name down on the housing list and one day the council wrote to me and I went down and picked the keys up. It had one bedroom and the bathroom was behind a sliding door in the kitchen. I was very excited and as pleased as punch. The flat was in a right rough block like a sort of tenement block. Some of the families living there were what you'd call problem families. Nowadays most of them would have had A.S.B.Os slapped on them.

When I first walked through the front door the place was rotten. There was thick dust and cobwebs everywhere. I cleaned it up and stripped all the walls and put up new wood chip wallpaper. I painted a couple of the walls chocolate brown and done the skirting boards and the doors the same colour, I added in a touch of beige and a shade of magnolia and the place looked like a palace or more like Willie Wonka's chocolate factory! Anyway, it was different and was clean and more importantly it was mine. I'd never wallpapered in my life. I didn't want patterned wallpaper up because that would have been too hard to match up and a job to get it up flat with no creases in it. The wood chip I did manage to stick up didn't look half bad even though it did look like Frank Spencer had put it up, but I tried and that's what counts. For furniture, I bought a settee, for a tenner, that turned into a bed off me mate. It was black plastic with a touch of the colour orange on it. I had some right funny tastes in them days but it was all about to change as a woman came into my life and my bachelor pad was about to be revamped.

CHAPTER TWO

SATURDAY NIGHT FEVER

I settled into my flat straight away and I got it all kitted out. Now all I needed was a bird in my love nest. The flat was getting quite a reputation for somewhere to come back to after the pub and clubs had closed. I had some wild nights there and I mean wild.

Most Friday and Saturday nights I'd go to the Tottenham Royal. It was a big Mecca type ballroom with plastic palm trees and ultra violet lights and a huge D.J. stand on the stage. You had to dress smart to get in and it was guaranteed there'd be trouble. It was a mixture of all sorts of people in there as they danced the night away to Tamla Motown and Soul music. Thursday and Sunday night were Under 21 nights so I'd try and get down there as much as possible.

Outside, when the place closed, it would then kick off, big time. The locals from the Tottenham area would fight with the lads from the

Highbury area and the idiots they had there as bouncers would stand back and watch it. There'd be running battles up and down the road and a couple of times the crowd would turn on the bouncers and they'd cop a good hiding.

In them days it was a white, rough area but nowadays it's a black and immigrant rough area. I think in them days the infamous Broadwater Farm Estate wasn't even built.

I then started going to a little night club over near Smithfield meat market called Lyndsey's. It didn't used to open till midnight but it was a nice little club which was compact. You'd get about 150 people crammed in there. The club was inside a hotel and if you went down in the lift to the club, the lift doors would open and you'd come straight out onto the dance floor. It was all very Austin Powers, baby. Over the course of a few weeks I got talking to a girl down there and she told me her name was Lesley. We were friends in a big crowd and I took her out a couple of times, and one night I took her back to the Chocolate Factory. Romance blossomed and I went out with her for three years and then we got married. I knew things weren't right because when I first took her back to the flat she looked around and commented on what good taste I had. She originally came from North London and was born and bred in Islington.

We had a big, white wedding with all the trimmings, the big reception, the lot. Here I was, 19 years of age and married. Mum and dad weren't too happy. I think they knew it wouldn't last and they were right. The marriage lasted just 6 months. Looking back we were just too young. Perhaps if we'd stayed just as boyfriend and girlfriend that bit longer, who knows, we may well still be together today. We had our honeymoon on the Isle of Wight. Only the best for my woman. No, we didn't go over there just for the day; we went for the week in a nice caravan on a nice site with a nice swimming pool. It was right on the beach. The wedding went well with the church and the reception packed to the rafters and it was the first wedding amongst my family where there hadn't been a punch up. There was no hint of any bother. It was in the back of my mind all day long that there was going to be trouble. My lot were just like Gypsies, they had the same mentality as travellers.

The marriage collapsed when I met someone else. The Punk rock scene had exploded in London and I just loved the music and got into it big time. I used to go to the concerts and buy the records and then one night I met a lovely little girl named Melody. Also I'd been friends with Johnny Lydon (Johnny Rotten) all my life. He lived opposite me in the same street in Islington. My family were poor and didn't have a pot to piss in but his family was even worse off. They were a very, very poor family. They used to paint their windows with black paint because they couldn't afford curtains and instead of milk on their cornflakes they'd have warm water. John's a couple of months older than me and we've always been good mates. I went through the whole Punk thing with him and one time he asked me to be the drummer in his Public Image band. I was more interested in pounding the Punks rivals, the Teddy Boys, than pounding a drum kit. It's funny how these things happen. As I became a teenager I lost touch with John. Then one night I was at a concert and got talking to a geezer and it was him, not Johnny Lydon but Johnnie Rotten. Neither of us could believe it. "Fuckin hell," he said, "I remember the Buglionis, they used to look after us. If we ever had any trouble then ya Uncle Peter would come and sort it out."

I ended up doing some work for Johnny and was at the gigs with him at 'The Rainbow' and up at Leeds and I also done bits of work for one of the other big Punk bands,' The Damned' and the Ska revival band

'The Specials'. I still see the Pistol's drummer, Paul Cooke, over at Stamford Bridge, as he's a fellow Chelsea fan. He's a good mate of mine. The other two, Steve Jones and Glen Matlock I weren't too keen on. To me The Sex Pistols were the greatest rock and roll band ever. I was meant to be on their well-publicized boat trip up the Thames, which the old bill for some unknown reason stormed on board and arrested them all, but I turned up late and missed the boat. The Lydons were a nice family and I got on well with John's brothers, Jimmy and Martin. His old mum, God rest her soul, was a lovely woman. I still speak to him now and it's nice to catch up on how he's doing and what he's been up to.

Anyway, me new bird was Melody who I met at Billy's Club in Soho. She used to stay at the flat with me. She was a nice girl who was right into the whole Punk thing. We were right into bands like 'Slaughter and The Dogs'. Their big singles were Cranked up Really High and Where Have All The Boot Boys Gone?" But when I found out they were from Manchester I went a bit the other way, and went off, of them Another Manc band were 'The Buzzcocks' who were quite good. I done all the Punk things like posing up the King's Road and fighting our rivals The Teds. I lived my life as a Punk. I became a full time Punk. I had red, blue, and green hair. Looking back, I did get stared at and got some right funny looks. But did I care? I didn't give a fuck.

I remember going over to Highbury to watch Chelsea and the old bill turned me away. They got me in between two police horses, lifted me up and marched me away. They told me in no uncertain terms not to come back.

The one thing the Punk scene done was freshen up the whole music scene. Before the Pistols, you had bands like 'Pilot' and 'The Bay City

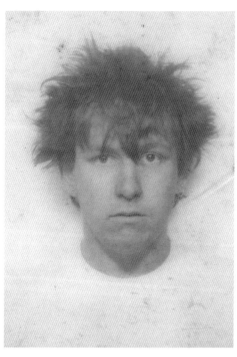

Just come out the hairdressers,
aged 22

Mum and Dad, Southend in the 50s

My Dad in his Army days

My Mum and Dad and both sets of parents

My uncles, Peter and Bernard with me

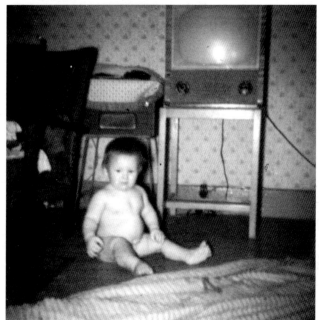

Me, 10 months,

Left to right:
Me, Jeffrey Day, a
friend , and my
brother Clifford

Me and Ralph

Me and Clifford in Hackney

Me and my brother, Ralph, aged about 23

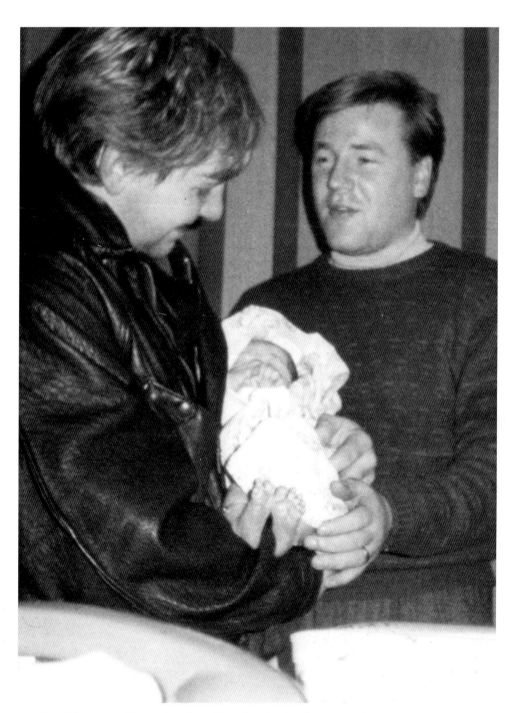

Ray Winstone with my daughter, Victoria, shortly after her birth

(*Facing page*) My wedding. What a waste of money; look at the clobber

In Cardiff for the Cup Final against Arsenal

Giles, Holte, and Terry

My mate Giles in Milan. Looks like he's just stepped out of Burtons window

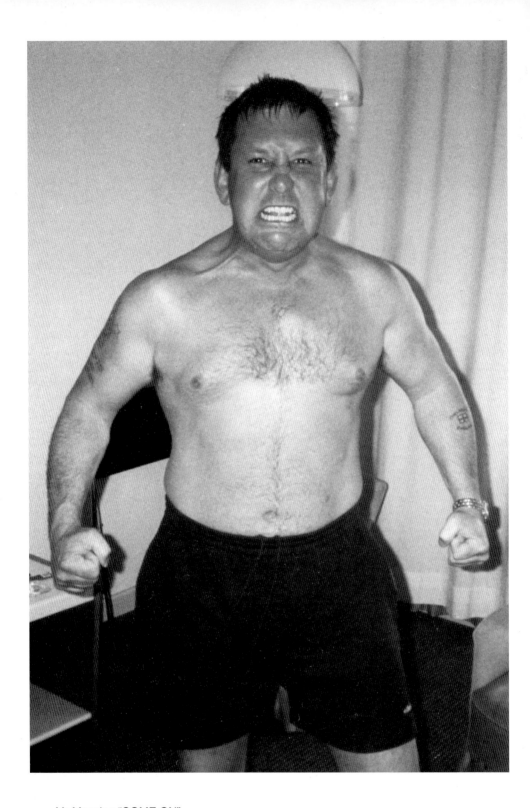

Mr Muscles "COME ON"

Milan, the "Ultras" set fire to their kitchen, cooking pasta

Stockholm with the boys

Lee, Cooper and my little Princess

Majorca, for the Cup Winners Cup – Semis

Me and Mr Sharp, a Chelsea fan and a mate of mine from North London

Me and Ray (middle) at the B.A.F.T.A. awards

Me and my Tottenham mate, Zac, outside the "British Lion" pub in Hackney Road

Dave and Ian.
Lewisham, at my
benefit do. All the
boys did me
proud that night

Kilburn.
and the boys ouside
"La Reserve"

Me and Ian Twin

Rollers', and 'Brotherhood of Man'. It was total crap, along with Soul and Disco. Popular music was dying on its feet.

Melody, and me were together for three years. We went into Punk together and we came out the other side together, when it finished. She even tried to get me to redecorate my flat but I loved the colour scheme. She did add a few feminine touches like slinging out the black and orange settee, but I wouldn't let her go too far. She did calm me down when we were together as there were no more mad mad nights at the flat. She did use to keep me out of trouble as well. As a Punk I tended to get into lots of fights.

The last fight I had, which finished it for me, was when a few of us Punks clashed with a group of Soul Boys outside the Camden Palace. We were watching 'Sham 69', which turned out to be one of their last gigs. The Soul Boys were throwing drinks and piss over us and we were just getting humiliated. About 10 of us went outside and waited for the Soul Boys and they came steaming out and just smashed the fuck out of us. I was fighting a losing battle in trying to keep the Punk movement going. I was on my own. It was sad. I should have realized we'd had our day and it had all been good while it lasted, but that battle at Camden was the final nail for me in the Punk coffin.

I was now so disillusioned by it all. Punk had even cost me my job working with my granddad. He gave me the sack till I grew my hair back to its natural colour. I was one divvey cunt. Being Italian he was very strict and he stuck by his word. He told me there was no way he'd let me work with him with my multi coloured hair. He said I'd be a laughing stock if I went onto a site looking how I did. He used to get the right hump. He just couldn't understand it. But Punk was now over.

I was earning 60 pound a week with me granddad and Melody got a job as a cashier in the post office, but even that didn't last and one day I came home from work and she'd left me. A scribbled note telling me that we were over was waiting for me. I had a feeling it was going to happen. When we first started seeing one another it was all lovey dovey and we were all over one another, but that might have been the booze and the speed and the weed making us feel that way about each other. We must have seen one another through a haze. As soon as the Punk thing was done and dusted and we dressed normal and got steady jobs she went and pissed off. Perhaps deep down we really didn't think that much of one another, although I do have Melody to thank for ridding me of my enstrangled wife.

I wasn't yet divorced from the old woman and one day I took Melody back to the Chocolate Factory not long after we'd met. We done a bit of gear and we both felt a bit amorous. Melody jumped in the bath behind the sliding doors in the kitchen and I was fucking about doing something or other. Next minute I heard these high heels come, clip clop, across the landing and the next minute the ex is standing in front of me. It was then the shit hit the fan. I told the old woman it was me mate in the bath but she wouldn't have it. She stormed off and I never saw her again. Later on I did hear she remarried and moved to the Isle of Wight. She must have liked the place from when we had our honeymoon over there. Less she met someone when we were on honeymoon and never told me, or perhaps she forgot to mention it to me? She might have fell in love with the skipper on the ferry on the way over from Portsmouth, come to think of it I do remember a geezer with a big white beard that kept on looking at her. You know the sort of Captain Birds Eye type.

Even when I was a Punk I never gave up going to football. Me and a few of the lads had a little firm called 'The Chelsea Punks'. In our heyday we would be 15 handed but we were a good little crew. Away from football, and before and after games we'd battle with The Teds up at Sloane Square. We'd steam into one another and you'd see the shoppers and the tourists scatter. We were a Japanese tourists dream. The Yuppies would drive past in their convertible Golf GTIs and look on in amazement. Mad, mad days that's all I can say.

Also I was on the move from the flat and got a three 3 bedroom town house just off the Essex Road in Islington. The council told me it was only two bedrooms but when I got the keys it turns out it was three bedrooms. Because one of the bedrooms had a boiler in it, it was classed as two bedrooms. Happy days!

I then met Gronia the new lady in my life who I stayed with for 21 years, and we had two beautiful daughters, Victoria and Alexandra. We never did get married but over the years we had some good times and some bad times, but she's the mother of my daughters so I aint going to slag her off.

CHAPTER THREE

AWAY DAYS

Just before I met Gronia I had a Chelsea tattoo on my arm and fuck me, did it hurt? Anyone that says tattoos when they've being done don't hurt are fucking liars. I thought I looked the dogs' bollocks with the Chelsea badge on my arm. I would stroll into the North Stand, that's where all the chaps went in those days, with a short-sleeved shirt on and show off my badge of honour.

In them days Hicky was running the show over at Chelsea, especially to away games up North where he ran 'Hicky's luxury coaches' to all sorts of far flung Northern outposts. He was infact a great bloke to know he was very well spoken with a great sense of humour. He'd have everyone in stitches with his stories and his exploits were legendary. I knew of him and had heard his name so many times before we actually met and it was at Bristol City away in about '79-'80 when I got to meet him.

A few of us were sitting in the seats on the side and Hicky came over to our group and said he'd arrange a row with the Bristol firm at half time. He said they were coming around to the Chelsea end and as it turned out they and he were true to his word. They came around half- time and we went straight into them and done them. We held them off at first and then we got the upper hand and smashed them. Some cunt was standing in front of me doing all the Karate moves like Bruce Lee, but I soon put paid to him with a cup of steaming hot Bovril in his face. Fuck all that Kung Fu lark.

After the game, it was a different story and it was our turn to get smashed. There were only about 30 of us, and as we came out, they were everywhere. We were surrounded and there was nowhere to go. It looked like we were about to be hammered. There was a bit of a stand off and then in seconds our whole end emptied out onto the street and now it was game on and it's now a different story as we back the Bristol firm all the way up the street.

After that, I went to every game, home and away. I even went to friendlies and a pre-season tour of Sweden where I ended up being deported. Me and me mate Germaine were on a boat from Hamburg to Sweden when we got involved in a fight with some Germans. We threatened to throw one of them overboard. When we arrived in Sweden, we didn't think no more of it and come off the boat and into passport control the old bill came from everywhere and we were marched off to a little side room to be questioned. We were then marched back onto the boat at gunpoint and sent back off to Hamburg where, on arrival, our passports were handed back to us. That was our Sweden trip. Two days to get there and two hours in Sweden before we were fucked off out of it.

Around '84-'85 I started hearing the name the Chelsea's Head-Hunters and to tell you the truth I didn't really take a lot of notice. It wasn't until years later that all the Chelsea firm got labeled with that name, and the tabloid press loved it. For them it had a certain ring to it. People from other clubs would ask me if I was in the Head-hunters and my reply was "No, I'm Chelsea North Stand." I mostly stood at that end of the ground where the away supporters congregated. I'd done my time in the benches and then the Shed. Now I was a North Stand boy and proud of it and ready for action.

We used to have a good firm in there and depending on who we were playing it would kick off. It took the old bill years to get clued up on the North Stand. Then it became away supporters only but that didn't stop us from trying to infiltrate it.

The police would have a line across the gates before you reached the turnstiles and they'd quiz anyone who looked a bit suspect on who they supported. Depending on who we were playing you've never heard so many bad Scouse, Manc or Brummie accents. If the coppers didn't like the look of you then it was a shove in the back and a "go on, fuck off up the other end." I've even seen genuine away fans turned away in total shock at the prospect of having to mix with us lot out on the street. There'd be crowds of young Chelsea faces hanging around like packs of wolves.

In those days, the old North Stand itself was still up and then for some reason or other it was pulled down. I don't know if it was for safety reasons but it never did look too safe. For those who don't remember it, it was in the old North Stand end of the ground where today you'll find the Mathew Harding Stand. To best describe it, it looked like a seating area on stilts; there were seats above and terracing underneath it. It was in the corner, right next to the old East Stand and covered about a quarter of the North Stand terrace. It was an odd looking piece of architecture.

Gronia was more understanding about me and football and what it meant to me more than any other previous girlfriend did. She never moaned about me going to football, well, not to me face. We originally met around a girlfriend's house who was just that, a girlfriend; she was a friend of a friend. We got chatting over a few drinks and it turns out she was an ex Punk rocker so we had a lot in common. We just hit it off and got on well. She was 6 years younger than me and you know what? she never had the pleasure of seeing Willy Wonkas Chocolate Factory. Instead, she moved into a bit of luxury with a three bed roomed town house. Later on we had two lovely daughters, Victoria was born in '85 and Alexandra was born in '88.

On the football front, I was going as often as I could. Derby County away in '81 was probably some of the worst violence I've ever witnessed at a football match. To put it politely it went fucking mental. About four or five thousand Chelsea, fans traveled up there, the majority by British Rail football specials. We came straight out of Derby station and found a pub and if I remember rightly, it was called 'The Victoria'. Anyway, that got wrecked. We just took the whole pub over. Someone found the key for the shed out the back where all the stock was kept so spirits and beer was being passed out, and handed around and drunk. Now every fucker was well oiled up. The bar staff couldn't work out why everyone's stumbling around drunk and yet no-ones paying at the bar for the bottles of beer and spirits they were drinking. Everyone was getting more and more drunk and the pub more packed as the word spread that The Victoria was the pub for a free drink. They had ornamental swords hanging on the walls and it wasn't long before they went missing.

Next thing the pub empties as word goes around that Tottenham are in town. Apparently, a mob of Spurs has stopped off in Derby on their way to Nottingham to play Forest and had slapped a few Chelsea Scarves. They didn't realize just how big a mob we had out that day but they soon found out as we found them on the platform of the station and smashed them to bits. They got mullered. They were running down the tracks to get away and one geezer locked himself in the station waiting room.

As we came out of the station, a mob of Derby appeared and came straight into us. It was one of the longest rows I've ever seen at football. It went on relentless for a good five minutes. People were being hit and either went down or carried on fighting. No one from either side took a backward step. The Old Bill just couldn't stop it. Finally, the two firms were pushed apart with; I'd have to say, the honours going to Derby.

Inside the ground, a few of us got into the home end and kicked it off. We stayed in there until just before half time and then the old bill moved in and slung us out and put us in with the rest of the Chelsea masses.

Afterwards it was going off everywhere as we were escorted back to the station. I'll give Derby their due they came into us at every opportunity. At every street corner, they'd make a stand and we'd roar across the road at them and then another mob of theirs would come from the other side of the street or from behind us. The Derby streets were only narrow with rows and rows of brick built terraced houses and the sound of rioting echoed through them streets that day. On that day's performance, I rate Derby's firm highly. There was only thirteen thousand fans at the Baseball ground for that game and Clive Walker scored for us and some geezer called Osgood scored for them. It wasn't the great Peter Osgood scoring an own goal but a Derby player named Keith Osgood. I wonder what ever happened to him?

Cambridge away was another game where we took huge numbers. Five of us drove from Romford and stopped in some little picturesque village outside of Cambridge. On the trip, that day was me, Germaine, Windmill, Wingnut and Doddy. We had a few beers and talked about football and what to expect of Cambridge's firm that day. A few of the boys doubted that Cambridge even had a firm. "Aint it all students on bikes dressed in black cloaks with mortar-boards on their heads?" one of the lads asked. The thing is little teams like ya Cambridge and Oxford and York and Hereford can pull good firms on their day and will always turn out for the big boys. They may not meet their visitors head on but they'd turn out and have a pop and do a quick Kamikaze attack. Teams like Cambridge couldn't go toe to toe with teams like us or Man Utd or Leeds or Spurs, but if there was fifty of them and fifty of us then they'd give a good account of themselves.

On the day we parked up near the ground and bumped into Hicky who'd run one of his coaches up there. It was agreed that we'd all pay to go into the home end and meet up at the back. We devised a plan that I'd make out that one of the boys was deaf and dumb and that I'd do all the talking. Outside the turnstiles under the watchful eye of the local constabulary, I tried my hand at some sign language. It worked and as I paid for both of us to get in and we sailed through without a hitch. Our mob was everywhere and within five minutes of mobbing up it kicked off. About ten of us got separated from the rest of the boys and we were having a right old battle down in the corner. Outside we swarmed all over them and gave the Cambridge leader, 'The General', a good hiding. Really, Hicky saved him from further punishment. He was on the ground nearly spark out. "Hang on lads, he's had enough" said Hicky. "No he aint" said a few of us. "He's a gobby cunt who deserves all he gets." How the fuck was this prick Cambridge's top boy? He was only in his early twenties, if that, and he had hardly any hair and he had a face like E.T. and was about as fat as a chip. The poor cunt didn't have a lot going for him. While we were arguing amongst ourselves, this little hobbit slipped away. He must of escaped unharmed because I've since seen him in The 'Lord of the Rings' film.

Near the exit Cambridge came back into us and the old bill, in a bit of a panic, closed the gates shut and a few of us were trapped inside the ground with their firm. Outside, on the other side of the gates the old bill was having a right job in holding the Chelsea hordes back from joining us. That was the first time I met Giles from Chelsea and since that day, we've been good friends. I know a few teams that have come unstuck at Cambridge. They have a game little mob.

Music wise, I fell out of love with it. It was the time of the new romantics with Duran Duran and Spandau Ballet being the new kids on the block. But they did nothing for me.

A funny story from our trip to Cambridge was of a local fisherman sitting on a brick bridge without a care in the world with his rod in his hand. It was very quaint and picture postcard. He looked very relaxed, as he sat just across the way from us. We could see him as we made our way into the ground and next thing some Chelsea fans have walked past him and gave him a shove in the back and sent him flying into the fast flowing waters. It was a miracle but he landed upright with his fishing rod still in his hand but the waters were lapping around his chin and he was in a bit of a panic. Next thing the old bill have turned up and in their attempts to rescue him a couple of them have slid down the muddy river bank and gone arse over tit straight into the water. Hundreds of Chelsea fans cheered and laughed as the "Keystone Cops" made a right balls up of their rescue.

In them days, we played teams like Wrexham and Preston, Orient and Grimsby. Life was shit in the old Second Division but us die-hard Chelsea fans were very loyal. It's a pity some of the players didn't have the same enthusiasm as us fans. One nice fixture in those days was a trip down to Cardiff. I rate them in the top ten firms in Britain. Over the years, they've had some right battles with their old rivals from the Den, Millwall.

For the game down there, a few of us met at Paddington station early and used our student rail cards and Persil vouchers to get train tickets. Suddenly a mob of about 100 geezers came marching across the station towards us. We knew they weren't Chelsea. "Is this ya firm Chelsea?" asked the huge, black geezer fronting this mob. "No," I said, looking around a bit nervously as there was only about 40 of us scattered around. "We're meeting up in Cardiff." "Right, make sure you're back here after the game as we've a few things to sort out," said the black bloke looking straight into my eyes and sounding as if he meant it. With that, they turned and strolled out of the station. "That was Cass and the I.C.F.," a couple of our boys said. They could have taken a few liberties as they well outnumbered us but I suppose they must have looked at it that we hadn't run when they turned up. What the fuck was they doing at Paddington at that time of the morning?

We found some seats on the first train down to Wales and cracked open a few cans of beer. We needed something to calm our nerves after that close shave. After that, what would Cardiff have waiting for us? We pulled into Cardiff Station and came out and walked across to the big pub right opposite. Once inside we met up with a few other faces who'd driven down. Things were looking a little better. We found a seat near the window and settled down with a beer. Outside we could see a few Cardiff spotters walking past and trying to have a sneaky look inside the pub.

The old bill hadn't sussed us yet and were nowhere to be seen. Next minute 150 Cardiff came towards the pub. The windows went in and they're bouncing up and down outside. We instinctively held the doors and they couldn't get in. We repelled their first attacks and then the old bill turned up and forced us out of the pub. The Cardiff lot stood on the other side of the road laughing. They weren't bothered at all about the old bill who pointed out to us that Cardiff's firm were across the road and warned us that if it went off again then they would step back and pick up the pieces.

Just then another train pulled in and 200 of our boys piled out onto the street. Up the front were the usual suspects, Hicky, Giles, Skitzy, Rutland and Ian from Lewisham. Now the only pieces the police would be picking up would be Welsh pieces.

We moved off as the old bill fucked off and left us to it. We came to a crossroads and 100 strong Cardiff mob met us head on. Through sheer weight of numbers, we ran them up the road. Now the old bill was back. They didn't obviously like what they were seeing. We came to a bridge and they came into us again. Up ahead we could see Ninian Park and again they came into us from three sides. Bricks and bottles came through the air at us. This was a violent attack and to be honest a few of our boys got done. We had nowhere to go and we couldn't back off. The old bill now took control and pushed Cardiff back up towards the ground. They then surrounded us and slowly marched us through the streets. Every now and again, the police escort would stop and the coppers at the front would clear a way through the crowds.

I'll give the Welsh lads their due. They took their fighting seriously and were well game. There were a few of our lot with split and cut heads and black eyes. As we queued to get into the ground we knew we'd been in a right old battle.

Inside the ground about 25 of our lot got tickets for the seats in their part of the ground. Cardiff sussed them out and came steaming into them from behind. The old bill rushed in, split it up, and put the Chelsea boys back in with us lot. After the game, it was a different story as thousands of us poured out onto the street. Cardiff knew they wouldn't make a dent in this lot and made a couple of half hearted attempts to get through the police lines at us. But the nearer we got to the station the smaller their mob became.

Back at Paddington, we pulled in and everyone quietly jumped off and moved towards the ticket barriers. There was no singing, no noise. If West Ham were waiting as they'd promised then they were in for a shock. To our disappointment, there was no welcoming committee from the East end and the solitary two coppers watching us arrive told the true picture.

In the return game at the Bridge, they never really showed and it was a non-event. But I did see Cardiff at Enfield in a Cup game and they smashed everyone and everything to pieces. They smashed the pubs, the shops, the ground. Anyone that got in their way got steam rollered.

Away from football, Gronia and me are getting on well. She's working as an art director on film sets and through her work, I meet the actors Ray Winstone and Clive Mantle. She worked on the film Robin of Sherwood and I got to go on set with her and go to a few cast parties and piss ups. Ray and me got on well, mainly because of our Hackney connections. Ray's a Hackney lad and we had a lot in common, even though he's a West Ham fan. Ray had done the 'Scum' and later a film with the Sex Pistols called 'All Washed Up', which, if I remember rightly, was a total flop. We got on really well, our families became very close, and we almost lived together. Ray had a place and we wanted to get one on the same estate. We'd let our place in Islington go and rented a house in Muswell Hill. That came to an end so we were in a hostel waiting to be rehoused.

The place in Muswell Hill was a penthouse flat and was costing us £200 a week a lot of money even back then. We let the good times go to our head. Well, Gronia was doing well at work and we just got a bit flash. Ray is very family oriented and suggested we move nearer to him in Enfield. I'm Godfather to his daughter and they're Godparents to my Victoria. In the end, we were offered 34, Weatherby Road and Ray lived at 32 in a maisonette but we turned it down because we would have literally been living in one another's pockets. "Take it" said Ray, "we'll knock the partitioning down and make it one big maisonette."

Ray's a great actor but he wasn't nice to everyone. Not in a horrible way. It's just in his nature and some people take his manner the wrong way. In Robin of Sherwood, he played Will Scarlet alongside Sean Connery's son. It used to be on T.V. every Saturday afternoon after the classified football results. One minute Ray was a nobody and had been chucked out of drama school for fucking about, and then Ray Clarke, well I think his name's Ray Clarke who wrote the original version of 'Scum' for the BBC, went down to the Anna Scher, Stage School in Islington and said he was looking for someone to play the part of a tear away, hard boy troublemaker and leader. They said they didn't have anyone on their books who would be suitable, but one of the teachers remembered Ray and said that he may be good for the part, even though he'd just been kicked out of the school. He got the part, Barry Norman gave him rave reviews on Film Night, and the rest so they say is history.

It was a bumpy and far from smooth ride up the ladder of fame as he used to get into a fair few scrapes. People would try picking on him and shout out bits of the film. "Where's ya tool?" and "I'm the daddy" were just a couple. In the end, he's only human and he would bite. You get loads of silly cunts making snide remarks behind his back but now he's learnt to rise above it. I've been everywhere with him, the best restaurants, the trendy clubs, the BAFTAS, Joey Pyles parties, and I've loved every minute of it. I've got a few pictures of Ray and me at one of Joe's parties, and we both look well plastered I'm so pleased Ray's done well because he deserves it and we're still great friends. I still go around his house and I pick up the phone and have a chat every so often. I'm well pleased for him and wish him even more success. He deserves it because he's worked hard to get to where his is.

CHAPTER FOUR

FISH, AND WE HAD OUR CHIPS

We took a few cans of beer and settled down to a game of cards and a more serious game of piss taking. Anyone that bit or copped the hump got it even more. It could be about your hair, your shirt, your shoes, and the remnants of toothpaste in the corner of your mouth, or your B.O. Or lack of deodorant. It could be anything but it was a laugh and a source of entertainment to relieve the boredom on long train journeys.

Today we were off to Grimsby to watch the mighty Blue Boys. By the looks of it, me, Prykey, Doddy and Skin were the only Chelsea fans on this train. Most, I suppose, had gone up earlier on the football special. We changed at Newark and then got on an old rattler to Cleethorpes. We must have stopped at 20 or more stations, on route.

We got off the other end at a near deserted station and found a pub, which wasn't exactly a hive of activity as inside was one old boy with a cloth cap on sat at the bar supping a pint, with a pipe hanging out the side of his mouth. He had a dog at his feet, which was bent over double licking its arse and bollocks. Could the day get better?

We drank up, walked along the narrow cobbled streets, and headed for the sea front. Fucking hell, this place was a ghost town. We saw a few fishermen, dressed in yellow oilskin suits, on their way back home after a nights work, but there was no young people or anyone that even slightly resembled a football fan. We found a fish and chip shop and this place seemed to have more life than the rest of the town. Even we got excited as we eat probably the best fish and chips I've ever had in me life.

Our big firm of four decided to head towards Blundell Park the stadium where Grimsby Town plays. We walked past a pub and this time it looked a bit more promising as there was seven Grimsby fans sitting at the window watching the world go by. As we walked in the place went silent. We ordered our drinks, and went and sat in the corner, skinned up, and smoked a few joints. That felt better now we'd been fed and watered. Still no sign of any other Chelsea fans and we all decided as we sipped our pints that it had been a long old journey just to watch a football match.

Donkey jackets and fishermen's wellies seem to be in fashion in Grimsby and the clobber we had on seemed to make people stare at us.

We walked off towards the ground or should I say floated off towards the ground as the weed had started taking effect.

The ground appeared around the next corner and a sign hanging on a rusty chain link fence informed us that it was "away fans to the right," so us being awkward bastards, went left and followed the few home fans that were about. We could see 'Findus' written on the roof of one of the stands and we laughed. This area must have been reserved for Captain Birds Eye look-alikes only, or worse birds with smelly minges. We queued up and got some strange looks from the locals. It wasn't in our blood to turn and walk away. We paid to get in and made our way out onto the terraces.

The Chelsea fans that had made the trip were packed behind the goal at the other end of the ground and they were in good voice. Meanwhile, it hadn't taken the locals long to suss us out and a small group stood behind us as we lent on one of the metal barriers having a coffee. "What a shit hole" said Doddy aloud? About 200 of their boys packed behind the goal in the middle of the terrace chanted "Grimsby, Grimsby." A few of them looked our way and pointed at us. I think they knew we were there and were strangers in the camp It was only a matter of time before we came under attack. We looked around hoping to catch sight of a few familiar faces. Perhaps a few of the Chelsea boys had had the same idea as us and had come into the home end.

In those days, Chelsea had a bit of a reputation for invading and taking ends. I felt like a boxer waiting to go into the ring. I had butterflies in my stomach and I could tell the others were worried because our idle, nervous chat had stopped. I also noticed a lack of policemen in this end, as they all seemed to be down the Chelsea end of the ground. Then I heard it. "Come on you Chelsea wankers, let's have it." I looked around and noticed their mob surrounding us had grown. They must have all gone to the same school as they all had on identical donkey jackets. "Come on you Southern wankers," said one big-mouthed cunt amongst them, traces of angry spit bubbling up on his pencil thin moustache that only Northerners think look trendy.

And then it went. They came down the terrace at us and my coffee went everywhere. Good job it wasn't Starbucks at three pound a cup. I would have had the right hump. A few of theirs hit the deck caught by a couple of good shots from Prykey and me. Doddy had been knocked down and it looked like he was out cold and in big trouble as he was getting kicked to the head and body. Skin dived in and sheltered Doddy as best he could but he was getting whacked and whacked and was getting weaker, and now he was in danger of going over.

I then heard the Chelsea fans singing "North Stand, North Stand, do your job" a song the Shed boys would sing when there was trouble at Stamford Bridge. The North Stand boys were seen as the real hardcore hooligans in those days but the truth was today we weren't really doing that good a job and in reality were getting a good hiding.

Next thing the Old Bill moved in and dragged us through the crowds and out of the ground. We were slung up against a wall and cautioned. We were told we had ten minutes to get as far away from the ground as possible. After that, if the old bill saw us again then we would be arrested. So, their best advice was to piss off and thank our lucky stars we hadn't been nicked.

We limped off licking our wounds as we heard the crowd roaring, which signaled the game had just kicked off. We stopped at the top of the road and checked if everyone was O.K. Without saying a word we knew each of us wanted revenge on these slags and we knew we didn't have to wait long because the gates to let fans leave early would be open twenty minutes before the final whistle. We knew going back into their end for revenge would be suicide so we devised a plan to plot up near some public toilets just outside the ground. So that's what we done. As soon as we heard the final whistle and a cheer go up, we knew we had to act quickly. Them cunts inside the ground had taken right liberties so now it was our turn to dish out a bit of punishment. However, we had to do it swiftly and get on our toes and have it away before we were collared by the local old bill.

Doddy couldn't wait to get started but in reality, he couldn't fight his way out of a paper bag; he just couldn't hold his hands up. He wasn't a lightweight; he was more a paperweight. He was more into arson and loved burning things and blowing things up. He was our explosives man who loved November the 5th. It was the same when he got put on his arse in the ground. OK we were getting chinned but he only got caught with one shot, which was no more than a girly slap, and he was out cold.

Three thuggish looking young men who looked like they were up for a row but in desperate need of a piss, approached the gents' toilets. Once inside we battered them. They didn't stand a chance. "Tell ya bully mates we're Chelsea" we said. It was pay back time and our exercise went like clockwork.

The Chelsea S.A.S. had carried out its mission behind enemy lines and were now off. We walked briskly back through the crowds as if nothing had happened. At the station, we met up with the rest of the Chelsea fans and boarded the train back to London. My leg was fucked and I had a black eye and a swollen lip. Doddy's ribs were killing him from the kicking he took, and Skin and Pryky had various cuts, lumps and bruises. I ached for days after that but it answered one question Doddy had asked on the train on the way up. "Do you reckon Grimsby's got a firm?"

After that, I never really saw Doddy a lot, although he did come to a few games, and then he disappeared. Doddy was a close friend of mine for years and years and then, as I say, he just disappeared. Maybe he grew up and decided to give it a rest. A couple of the lads reckon he may have died and we never heard. I think when my daughters were born and when my wife left me then he would have got in touch, as we were very close. Personally, I think he's no longer with us but if he is still around and he reads this then get in touch mate. It's been a long time but I'd love to hear from you. Perhaps he's playing cards somewhere with Lord Lucan or working in a fireworks factory in China. Now that would be right up his street.

I still see Pryky and Skin and they still go to football but Skin's wife won't let him come with me in case I get him into trouble. They still live over in Essex but out of all that lot its only me and me pal, Copper that go with the firm.

CHAPTER FIVE

FRIDAY NIGHT GAMES

Around this time I chalked up my first football related conviction as I got nicked for threatening behaviour after a game with Notts County. How the fuck can you get nicked against Notts County? Forest yes, but Notts County? What was I possibly thinking of? For some reason, over a period, Chelsea played a few games on a Friday night instead of the usual Saturday afternoon.

One such game was Barnsley away. I don't think they changed it for television purposes, I think the F.A. were just giving the Friday night fixture a bit of a trial. I'd come across Barnsley's firm at an F.A. Cup game between them and non-league Enfield, which was played at Spurs, White Hart Lane stadium. Enfield turned out a good firm but not good enough to take on and do Barnsley.

The usual suspects of me, Doddy, Skin and Prykey got the train from

London on Friday lunch time and decided to stop off in Sheffield before carrying on by train to Barnsley. Once in Sheffield we found a typical Northern pub, which was in desperate need of some modernizing and a bit of decorating. Inside it had the usual dartboard, fruit machine and of cause no one in it. We had a couple of pints and a puff and then wandered back over to the station. To our surprise, we spotted a mob of about 15 Barnsley fans on the look out for Chelsea fans like us who were changing trains. There was only four of us so we gave them a swerve and got on the train to Barnsley.

Next thing the Old Bill have turned up with dogs and ordered us off the train and onto the platform, where they searched us. They informed us that we'd been stopped because we'd been seen provoking Barnsley fans and hurling insults at them outside the train station. We all looked at one another in disbelief. As they were holding us the last train to Barnsley, which we'd been sitting on pulled out of the station. "You've got two choices," said one of the coppers. "You've got 20 minutes to fuck off out of Sheffield or you get the next train back to London."

Prykey came up with the idea of catching a coach to Barnsley so that's what we did. The coach ride was only about half an hour from Sheffield and we managed to grab a few beers to take on board with us. Things were looking up. We sat up the back of the coach like naughty schoolboys and as the beer flowed, we got a little drunk and a bit noisy. There was only about 10 people on the coach. Be fair, who in their right mind would want to go to Barnsley on a Friday night?

In front of us sat two fellas who looked like football fans. We started singing all the old Chelsea songs and after a while, one of these blokes started to get the hump, was muttering under his breath about us being scum and pond life, and should grow up. I did no more than punch him straight in the back of the head. "Take that you cunt," I said as his mate jumped up and demanded the driver stop the coach, and call the police. The bloke who I punched had a bit of sense to calm his mate and the situation down, and the coach carrried on into Barnsley bus station, with no more bother.

The game had already kicked off when we arrived and after a short walk, we could see the grounds' floodlights lighting up the dark, Yorkshire sky. The streets were deserted and then out of a side street, looking lost, came half a dozen fellow Chelsea fans. As we got to the ground, our newfound friends went and paid to get in the Chelsea section. We, being a bit more daring and out for a bit of revenge after the Enfield game, decided to go in where the home supporters were congregated.

We paid to get in with no hassle and walked down the terraces until we came to a metal fence that separated the Chelsea fans from the Barnsley fans. It took the Barnsley fans all of a minute to suss us out and we got heaps of abuse. "You cockney wankers, fuck off out of here," was only one of the shouts hurled at us. Then coins were coming from behind us and skimming over our heads. "Fucking hell," I said, "we've got to get out of here." Skin and Doddy made the first attempt to scale the fence and to escape but just as they held onto the bars and began to pull themselves up, then it started. Barnsley's mob came hurtling down the terraces at us. The first wave came into us kicking and punching. We had nowhere to go and all we could do was fight. We had our backs to the fence and behind us the Chelsea hordes pushed towards us from their section. But to be honest there was nothing they could do to help us. For some reason the Barnsley onslaught subsided for a few seconds and they backed off and gave a couple of yards space between them and us.

Two plain-clothes coppers and four-uniformed Old Bill grabbed us and dragged us up the terrace and through the Barnsley mob. We were being kicked and punched and spat on as the crowd parted like the Red Sea and the police threw us up against a wall outside. It was name and address time and then an escort back to the station.

We were then told if we didn't leave town then and there we would find ourselves locked up in the police cells for the weekend. What is it with Northern Old Bill and Chelsea fans?

We sat on the station platform well pissed off. We'd come here for revenge and all we'd done is come unstuck at yet another Northern dreary outpost. Then Doddy came up with what he thought was an amazing idea. His plan was to book into a hotel or B and B and when all the crowds and the police had gone, then we'd sneak out of the hotel at about four in the morning, and burn the ground down. At the time, it sounded like a good idea but we soon dismissed it as a bit too extreme and just a touch over the top.

Ignoring the Old Bill's threat to bang us up we decide to walk back down to the ground. At the turnstiles, we told the old boy on the exit gate that we'd arrived late from London as our car had broken down on the motorway and we had to leave the car and walk to the ground. Instantly he opened the gate and waved us in. "Come on in lads, it's the least I can do." Fucking hell, someone with a bit of compassion. "Cheers mate," we all said, as we trooped in, proud that our cock and bull story had worked.

The game was well into the second half as we looked around the fifteen hundred or so Chelsea supporters that had made the long trip but, by the looks of it, we didn't have much of a firm but you never could tell with our support. At the first sign of a punch up the shirts and the 'Shed boys' could sometimes be the first ones in.

At the end of the game, the police held us back inside the ground for ten minutes and when they thought it was safe for us to leave, they opened the exit gate and we swarmed out onto the street. It was pitch black but almost immediately, we could make out a mob standing directly in front of us. This firm came straight into us with fists and boots flying. We just stood firm and gave as good as we were getting.

An almighty push from behind sent a tidal wave of Chelsea fans into the Barnsley mob. There was no way, even if we had of wanted to, to stop it. It was like a dam bursting as a sea of bodies flowed forward. We had the Barnsley firm on the move as we chased them all the way back around the main stand. The Old Bill moved in and started nicking a few people. How else was the money going to be raised to pay for the policing on the night? A few thousand pounds through the courts and into the police coffers might well help. I think the police call it processing. Nick as many people as you can, get them in court for any reason, and fine the fuck out of them. Good old British justice at its best? It was funny on the night I didn't see many Barnsley fans getting their collars felt.

The police took control and it looked like it was all over. We'd done well and had given a good account of ourselves. A lot of the crowd started to dwindle and wander off in different directions. Some headed for the nearest pub, others off to their cars for the long drive back south, and a few headed for the railway station. We could sense we were being followed so a few of us, who were up for a row, dropped back. A fight started across the road and a few Chelsea got run. Up ahead another row started and again a group of Chelsea fans got scattered.

We crossed the road towards the trouble and a group of Barnsley was standing on a street corner. Without a word, Skin chinned one of them and put him on his arse. That was the signal for the rest of them to bolt. A few more Chelsea came across the road to back us up. These weren't major players, just normal fans I'd seen at a few games. I hadn't seen any of our main faces here tonight. No Hicky, no Babs or Eccles. He'd long since retired. Rumor had it he was out in Rhodesia fighting in a mercenary unit, a real life Dog of War.

Up ahead of us now was more trouble with a few Chelsea fans being chased back towards us but the old bill got in between the two sets of fans and pushed the Barnsley fans towards us. Now it was game on. We fanned out across the road in an attempt to make our firm look bigger. The Barnsley mob stopped and it seemed unaware how to deal with us. We took the initiative and steamed straight into them. This time they stood and came straight into us. I don't know what happened to the rest of the lads with us but again it was down to us four. Skin in his anger disappeared into the centre of the Barnsley firm. Next thing a copper's released his dog from its lead and the first arse it's seen to have a chomp on was poor old Skin's. It ripped his jeans and his skid marked pants and exposed his bare buttocks as it pulled him to the floor but I give Skin his due, he wasn't just lying there and letting the dog have all its own way. He was punching the fuck out of it as they rolled around on the floor W.W.F. style. Hulk Hogan or should I say Skiddy Skin was then carted off.

As we stopped momentarily to watch all this, some Barnsley cunt's sneaked up beside me and cracked me up the side of the head with one powerful punch. The force of the shot knocked me down but before any of them could move in to finish me off Prykey came to my rescue and whacked one of their main boys. This gave me time to get to my feet and off we went again, back into them. The old bill moved in on horseback and the rest of us slipped away.

We sat on the station for ages waiting for a train and within earshot was a group of Chelsea fans boasting loudly of how they'd just run Barnsley's firm. The bollocks they were spouting made my blood boil and I pulled the mouthy one amongst them and told him a few home truths. In the end, I just lost it and gave him a slap. I was so fucking angry.

Skin went to court back in Barnsley a few weeks later and received a £500 fine for threatening behaviour. He appeared in court under his real name, David Hayling, or Alien as some people pronounced it. He got the name of Skin simply because at one time he was a Skinhead. All in all it was a Friday night to remember.

Another Friday night game was Exeter in a friendly down in the West Country. I went down on the train on my own because my lot didn't fancy it. I thought, "fuck it." I finished work early and so off I went. I met my mate, Scotty from Taunton, on the train and we headed to the nearest pub to the station. As soon as we walked in the pub was full with a big mob of Chelsea. I looked around and saw Greenaway and Buggsy from Maidstone. Now I felt good knowing there was some good boys down there. Buggsy was well handy and well game and over the years, I've seen him put a few people down. In the last few years, he's another one that seems to have disappeared.

On the night we just took the piss, a few of our boys went into the Exeter end and cleared it, and we cleared the off license outside the ground of all its stock. It was a lovely summers evening and we sat on the terraces watching football and drinking. Life couldn't get much better.

After the game we headed down the waterfront to the Quayside and that's when all the trouble started. Big Colin from Wembley threw a bouncer through a plate glass window. It just went mental. We weren't fighting with football fans but the locals. We was a bit powerful that night and even the old bill left us alone. We didn't see them all night until a few nightclubs started getting smashed up and a few bouncers copped hidings. We were rounded up and put in the station and put on the first milk train or mail train or whatever they used to call it.

I'm sure it was at that game that I first heard the Chelsea song, "One man went to Mow" sung. I heard Greenaway singing it a couple of times that night. I'd never heard it before and thought it was a strange song for a football crowd to sing. Greenaway used to love singing it and used to do all the actions. Over the years, Greenaway became Mr. Chelsea and was a legend at Chelsea but he sadly died in 1999. His Zigger Zagger chant could be heard across the terraces at most grounds and he was the original leader of The Shed.

Exeter turned out to be a good day out and I really enjoyed myself. Leicester was another Friday night game where there was some real big serious rows. Leicester's mob tried to ambush us in some flats near the ground. They tried and failed to corner us after the game. We came out at the final whistle and clashed with a few of their boys. They ran off, and we chased them into some flats and waiting for us was a huge mob of Leicester and now it looked as though we'd been caught in their trap. But we had some serious boys in that firm and we set about smashing them to pieces. Before the game there was the usual little, stand offs, and scuffles and a few of us jumped into cabs to lose the old bill.

Before the game, we tried to take their end and a smoke bomb was thrown. After all that, I rate Leicester and think personally they've got a tidy firm. But the one thing against them is that they don't travel. They've never been to Chelsea with a firm and there's no two ways about it. As an away mob, they're shit but at their place, they're a handful.

I've also been up there when about 10 of us were fighting with them, they were coming into us from every direction, and we were bullied and terrorized. Every time we've gone up there with a firm, I've never seen them do us. One time up there, and for some unknown reason we didn't turn out a firm, they were out and about taking a few liberties.

I saw them running down side streets bottling people and hitting people, not firm just normal supporters. I have heard that Tottenham go up there and turn them inside out so too do West Ham. I think most of the London clubs go up there and do well.

Man City away was another Friday night game. Manchester was just full of Chelsea. We were everywhere. People went there by train, coach and car. There was thousands upon thousands of us up there that night. We were neck and neck with Sheffield Wednesday for the old Second Division title. In the run in, we beat Palace away 1-0 with a Pat Nevin goal. We then beat Shrewsbury comfortably 3-0 at home, then drew 2-2 with Pompey at Fratton Park in a midweek game. The following Saturday we thrashed Leeds 5-0 at home and smashed their mob to pieces at Piccadilly.

Next up was Man City and goals from Nevin and Dixon saw us win 2-0 in front of nearly twenty two thousand people, most of them Londoners. Micky Francis, Man City's main man who, by the way is no mug, got it 100% right in his book 'The Governors.' It was a true account of what went on that night. Chelsea just dominated that night. Before, during and after the game we were The Governors. A big flag was unfurled during the game, which was live on T.V. and it read, "Bring on Spurs" or words to that effect. We had one big massive firm out that night and I'd put the numbers as anything from a thousand to fifteen hundred.

The Old Bill couldn't really control it and Man City's firm knew this. We walked past a City pub and their firm was drinking outside. They saw us coming and walked back inside. They just didn't want to know. Every team has a dark day in the history of its firm or supporters. This was Man City's.

The next time we bumped into Man City's firm it turned out another bad day at the office for them. Chelsea were playing up at Oldham in a Division Two game and Man City were playing in an F.A. Cup semi final game, I think down at Villa Park. We went by train from London to Manchester Piccadilly and from there; it was just a short hop by train to Oldham. At Manchester Piccadilly, the place was swarming with City fans excited about their semi final trip. We got to Oldham, gave the police escort the slip, and found a little back street boozer. Inside the pub was a group of about 20 Chelsea and we had the usual chat about had we seen their mob? Did they even have a mob?" A local drinking in there and overhearing our conversation informed us that in fact, Oldham did have a firm and they were well game and could be well up for it. They'd tangled with Preston and Carlisle and Bury and Stockport in the past. "Wow," said one of the boys, taking the piss, "They've had some major rows."

Time was getting on and there was only about 15 minutes to kick off so I said to Doddy "Come on son, drink up. Let's fuck off out of this shit hole." He nipped to the toilet to have a piss and I finished the rest

The tattoo on my back

Me and Mark Cator, a good mate of mine

Under arrest for war crimes at football

Stamford Bridge, the view from my bedroom window

Napoli, home of pure Italian football

Arsenal's Denton, Chris Grainey and me

Me, playing for West Ham's Celebrities team before they became Chelsea's feeder club

Leicester City, away on a Friday night. Seconds later we charged their end

(*Facng page*) The Chelsea Youth – the future?

Tony Covelle

Me and Fat Pat

Victoria with the Premiership trophy, note the Head-Hunter scarf!

Me, Ray and two dolly birds

(*Facing page*) Panthers day out on the coast

Me and Ray at Joey Pyles party

Daddy's girl at The Parade 2006

of my pint. Someone at the bar has ordered three pints and half way through pulling the second the barman's dropped the glass as he noticed smoke bellowing from the mens' toilets. He rushed to the phone and called the fire brigade.

We were out of there in a flash and stood on the corner a couple of hundred yards up the road. Quite a crowd gathered. I suppose nothing this exciting ever-happened in Oldham with its drab, mostly boarded up, and terraced ram shackled housing. "Come on Bully, let's go back and see what we done," says Doddy as thick black smoke bellowed from every orifice of the pub. "We?" I said "don't you mean you?"

We fucked off a bit lively and headed towards the grounds floodlights, which were up in the distance. An old boy told us it was quicker if we were off to the football to cut across some wasteland he pointed to. Were the old folk of Oldham going to ambush us? Was this the leader of Oldham's over 60s, who were scheming a cunning plan? West Ham had their "under 5s! Maybe the mob geezer had spoke about in the pub was this pensioner gang, in for a penny, in for a pound, so we cut across the wasteland and the old fella was right. In no time we was at the ground, safe and well.

A couple of thousand Chelsea had made the trip and they were up to the usual of clumping any home fans that looked like they might be up for a row. It was cold, wet and windy so we quickly got inside the ground. After 10 minutes of watching a shit game, we had a wander about and met up with Chris from Battersea and about 20 of his mates. Someone suggested we leave about half an hour before the end of the game and wait back at Manchester Piccadilly for Man City to come back?

Back in Manchester 30, eager faces scanned the arrivals board and there it was. "Manchester City Football Special – Delayed." We couldn't believe our bad luck. It looked like there'd be no fun for us today. We pondered on waiting for the rest of the Chelsea or even plotting up in a nearby pub for City to come back, and then the decision was taken out of our hands as a couple of old bill on seeing us loitering about, rounded us up, and asked us where we was going too. They didn't get a sensible answer from any of us so they put us on the next train back to London.

We sat on this train for ages and it didn't move. The coppers stood on the platform making sure that we stayed on the train. One stood a few yards from the half open window with his back to us. We were well pissed off. Our little plan had been scuppered. Then a police radio crackled into life. "To all police units the first of the Man City football specials will arrive in exactly 5 minutes." As he told his colleague, we got up from where we were sitting, moved as one along the train, and opened the door at the front of the train without alerting the Old Bill. We jumped down onto the platform and moved silently and quickly up some stairs and onto a bridge that connected the platforms. At the top, there must have been forty of us crouching on our hands and knees. The Chelsea Commandos were ready for action as the train for London pulled out of the station, minus us, and the old bill, were still none the wiser.

We waited and waited in total silence and then suddenly we heard a train pull in below us and then with the echoing sound of doors opening and slamming the station filled with singing and chanting. Our adrenaline kicked in. The thing was they were facing the opposite way to us as they headed towards the ticket barrier so we were coming from behind so we had that element of surprise in our favour. But there was only about 40-50 of us, max and there was a good 600 of them. A chant went up, as we stood up and moved towards them, "Chelsea, Chelsea, Chelsea," and it echoed around the inside of the station. It sounded like there was 500 of us, not just 50. A few of their back markers got punched and then panic set in and within seconds we had their whole mob on the move. One geezer with a Union Jack flag hung over his shoulders with "Kippax Rules" on it, ran across the rail lines to get away. In the end, lots of them were jumping back onto the train they'd just arrived on and were opening the doors and jumping out the other side. We were tripping them up and clumping them and in the end, we cleared the station. I'm not saying this was by any stretch of the imagination Man City's main firm but a small group of us with good planning and being vastly outnumbered had caught another group of fans on the hop.

The old bill went fucking mad and questioned how we had managed to get back without being seen. No one was nicked but this time they kept a more than careful eye on us until that train was well under way.

About two hours into the journey the train slowed down to a snail's pace and then stopped. Some looked out of the window to see what the problem was and said that there was smoke coming out of the back carriage. Fuck me if it wasn't that bastard Doddy up to his old tricks. We arrived back in London about 4 hours late after the small fire was put out and then we were allowed to carry on back to London. That cunt Doddy just didn't know when to stop.

CHAPTER SIX

BLOOD BROTHERS

Overall, Chelsea, and Sheffield Wednesday have got on well over the years. Because of the England connections between Chelsea's Fat Pat and Wednesday's Sesh and Flynie, the two clubs as I say, don't have any axe to grind. Unlike Wednesday's rivals Sheffield United who both Chelsea and Wednesday hate with a passion.

To me United are a two bob outfit that, like Leicester, have never cut it at Chelsea. They're not bad at home, I'll give them their due, but away from Sheffield, they're shit and that big mouth, Cowans doesn't do them any favours. He talks a good fight and again, like a lot of Northerners, and he's grown one of them silly moustaches that the untrendy Scousers seem to favour.

I've spoken to a lot of the serious faces at Sheffield United and they've all said that all Cowans ever was was a bit part player. Anyone reading his book would know that. Two pages in and I realized the geezer was a dick. Who would put their wedding photos in a hooligan book? What's going to happen next in his follow up a family photo at his Nan's Ruby wedding? He's a 100% nob-head. I saw him on the 'Football Factory' documentary recently and he's as fat as a pig he can hardly move let alone fight he couldn't fight sleep, and as for sorting someone out, he couldn't sort out his laundry basket.

Sheffield Wednesday away in about '81-'82 was a day to remember. We met up late at my house and ended up missing the football special so we had to pay full whack and get an Inter City train up there. It was already getting on for eleven and the game kicked off at three. The train journey is about two and half, three hours, so we were cutting it fine. The good thing was the train had a buffet car so we could buy some cans of beer, which would make the journey that bit easier.

We found a first class compartment and me, Prykey, Doddy and Skin stretched out and made ourselves comfortable. It wasn't long before we got into a bit of a drunken haze and the conversation turned to the fights and the scrapes we'd been in together over the years. After a while, stupidly, someone suggested we become blood brothers. Doddy then laughed and said he had a better idea and was off to the toilet. He then pulled his lighter from his pocket and all of us knew what he meant. With that we all jumped on him and wrestled him to the floor and we wouldn't let him up until he promised not to do anything silly.

He calmed down and sat in the corner like he was sulking. We ignored him but kept our eyes on him. "Come on," said Skin, "let's become blood brothers." One of the boys produced a flick knife and Skin, who suggested the idea, gave himself a small nick on his thumb and out trickled some blood. I went next and on my own admission,

I went a little too hard and a little too deep as I still have the scar to this day. After me went Prykey and his was more of a scratch than a cut. Nevertheless, he did produce some blood.

The knife was then passed to Doddy. He looked at it, looked at the palm of his hand, went whack, and stuck it, point first, deep into the palm of his hand. Fucking hell, it was like a fountain as the blood spurted into the air. You could see the pain on his face and he'd caught his wrist so there was blood pissing everywhere. I pulled a headrest towel off the top of the seat and wrapped it around Doddy's hand. Straight away, it turned from white too red. Doddy was sitting there almost in shock. He wasn't saying a word. We could see by the amount of blood that he had made a mistake. By the looks of it, he would need stitching. I went to the toilet, got a whole bog roll, and wrapped it around his hand. Next came the linen towel but whatever we done nothing could stop it.

For the last twenty minutes, Doddy laid flat out with his arm raised in the air to try to stop the flow of blood, his face an ashen white. When we arrived in Sheffield, we jumped straight into a cab, not to the hospital but straight over to Hillsborough for the game. We were running late.

This was the first time in donkey's years that we'd been inside the ground before the game had kicked off. As we are queuing to get into the ground, spots of thick, congealed blood was forming at Doddy's feet. Even the Old Bill asked if there was a problem but we fobbed them off with a story that we were going to go straight to the first aid post.

Now Doddy had gone a funny shade of grey and green and we was all bothered about his health. He wasn't saying a lot and then just as the half time whistle went he lent forward and collapsed in a heap. The St. John ambulance men arrived, picked him up, put him on a stretcher, and wheeled him away around the side of the pitch. His clothes were soaked with blood and we were now very concerned for our blood brother. We followed closely behind as the ambulance men picked up the pace and took a short cut across the pitch. They knew he wasn't looking too good. Now we were shitting ourselves. I was thinking, "Please Doddy don't die. I know you can be one horrible little cunt at times but you don't deserve this." A hundred things were racing through my mind. Outside the stadium, he was put into a waiting ambulance and whisked off at speed. We weren't allowed to go with him in the ambulance to the hospital and the only information they would give us was that he was in a bad way, and they didn't know to which hospital he'd been taken to.

The second half of the game, was more of a blur than usual, this time it didn't come from booze or puff, we couldn't get our heads around the football, so we left the ground and made our way back to the station, very concerned about Doddy. All this and the game was still going on as we climbed on board a train back to London minus our old sparring partner Doddy. As the booze and the events of the day drained us, a couple of us began to doze off. One thing was, if we did fall asleep we didn't have the added worry of being woken by the train being on fire.

On the Monday, morning I found out that Doddy was O.K. and that he'd had five stitches put in his wound and that he'd needed blood. Doddy's real name was Michael Guy Dodkins and he was born on November 5th, Guy Fawkes night, hence is middle name Guy. His mum was a bit funny a sort of strange hippy woman and chose his middle name. An arsonist named Guy? You couldn't make it up could you?

After a good few years of struggling in the old Second Division, we finally got promoted back to the big time. John Neal the then Chelsea manager and I personally believe one of the best we've every had, put together a squad which in my view was the dogs bollocks. We had Kenny Dixon, David Speedie and fellow Scot, Pat Devin up front. Nigel Spackman and Micky Thomas in midfield and the experience of Welsh mad man Joey Jones at the back. That season, '83-'84 we went up as champions just pipping Sheffield Wednesday on goal difference for the title.

Back in the then top flight First Division, we kicked off with a Saturday morning game against Arsenal at "The Library" where the game ended in a 1-1 draw with Kerry Dixon getting our goal. We then beat Sunderland at home 1-0 and then lost to Everton 1-0. Now Everton fans have never really had a happy time visiting Stamford Bridge. Their team may have done well and nicked a few good results but their fans haven't faired too well on their trips to Chelsea. It's been well documented on the Chelsea ambush of Everton at High Street Kensington tube station. But how comes it happened? Was it an arranged meet? No one seems to know the answer, but as I said before, every club has a dark day in its history and this was Everton's.

After the game, Chelsea fans had been hanging around Earls Court station for the Everton fans to come through on their way back to Euston station. Next thing everyone's boarded a train to High Street Ken, because news had come through that Everton fans were boarding a train at Fulham Broadway which was taking them to High Street Ken. How the fuck did someone, find that out? This was pre-mobile phone days. Was it guesswork? Anyway, it ended up with Chelsea smashing Everton's firm to pieces and the underground having to be shut down as Everton fans fleeing the scene disappeared up one of the tunnels designed for tube trains and not for Scousers with cheap perms and silly moustaches, on foot.

Another ambush that went to plan was against Newcastle down at 'The Bridge.' During the game, word went around that we were going to ambush the Newcastle coaches as they left West London. We left the ground 20 minutes before the end of the game and headed for Wandsworth Bridge. When we arrived there was already a good 50 blokes there, armed with bricks, bottles and stones. As the game ended the crowd with us grew to a couple of hundred. We were all hiding down near the roundabout on the south side of the bridge. The Colonel of Terror had organized this and had done a brilliant job. When the Geordies arrived in their coaches they were stopped in their tracks by a hail of missiles and the windows were smashed and the coaches boarded and terrorized.

The following season we took a piss poor mob up there and the Geordies wanted revenge. After the final whistle the whole ground never moved and sang "Chelsea Must Die, Chelsea Must Die." They stayed behind for a good half an hour and sang their hatred of us. After the game if it wasn't for the Old Bill I'm sure there would have been fatalities. The Geordies were spitting blood and it was our blood they were after.

CHAPTER SEVEN

THE YOUTH CUP

How many football fans go to watch their own clubs youth games? Not many I can tell you, so when a mob of West Ham turned up for a semi final game in the F.A. Youth Cup it was quite a shock. About 30 of us were drinking in the pub opposite Stamford Bridge not expecting any trouble or to see any West Ham firm, when West Ham came bowling along taking liberties. The Chelsea fans in the pub were mostly normal supporters that were mad on Chelsea and took in all the club's games, be it, first team, reserves, the youth team, or a friendly, so they were, your not so normal anoraks.

West Ham was put in the East Stand lower and gave it plenty of mouth all through the game. We were stood in The Shed end talking to them through the fence. "Go and get your firm Chelsea, go on, you've got time, we aint going nowhere." They were about 70 handed and right gobby cunts. It spread like wild fire at the next home game that West Ham had come over for the youth team game and had taken the piss. Now we had to get our arses in gear and hatch a plan for the 2nd leg over at their place.

On the day of the game we arranged to meet early afternoon at a pub in Victoria. By 2 o'clock there was ten of us but it was a good ten. There was me, Hicky, Giles, Buggsy and a few of the youngens. Hicky said if we didn't have a 300 strong firm to go over there with then we could forget it and as he said that someone else turned up and that made the firm eleven. If we hadn't of laughed then we would have cried. Things were looking bad. Then a few more showed then Romford Lee, Doddy and Prykey showed up and then some more youngsters. Our numbers were swelling.

At 6 o'clock a decision was made to go over there and give it our best shot. We went down onto the platform of the East bound District Line and Giles had a count up and to our surprise there was 82 of us in total. We had no old bill with us so we had no back up if it came on top. All weapons were thrown in the platform rubbish bins as we thought we might well get stopped and searched at the other end. Reluctantly we were traveling across to the East End clean. Hicky pointed out that we didn't need them. "Let's go and do it the right way," he said, and he was right.

All of us squashed into one carriage and at every stop along the way we expected the train to stop, the doors to open and a mob of West Ham to be waiting looking at us on the platform. We passed Mile End and nothing. Now we were buzzing. I was thinking if we get there without having a row before Upton Park then we might just pull this off.

We reached Plaistow, another notorious I.C.F. haunt. Again, nothing, fuck all the place was deserted. The train doors shut. Next stop Upton Park. We pulled in, stood on the platform Hicky got everyone together, and we let everyone else, commuters, shoppers, and Joe public leave the station. I'll give Hicky his due he was a fantastic organizer. He was second to none. He was a very funny, articulate, educated person. He wasn't a nutter. He was a thinker and an organizer who had a certain way about him, and he was liked by everyone. He could move a 300 strong firm from one part of the country to another without being tumbled by the old bill. He was clever at what he done. It was all a laugh to him and he wasn't one of those nasty bastards. Don't get me wrong, he wasn't soft; he just didn't take himself too seriously.

We went up the stairs and through the barriers and bounced out into the streets. We turned right and on our right was the Queen's Pub. A mob of West Ham suddenly burst out the doors and came towards us. "I.C.F., I.C.F.," they chanted and we walked towards them doing the old "Hoo, Hoo, Hoo," Zulu noise. They had a big, black geezer at the front and a few of ours pointed him out as Cass. I didn't know him from Adam so I don't know if it was him or not. Anyway, someone's chinned him and he's gone backwards. We charged them and ran them back in the pub where they stopped at the doors and held us from getting right inside.

The old bill arrived from nowhere and pushed us across the other side of the road. The Queens has emptied again and about 40 West Ham were giving it large across the other side of the street. We ignored them as they had had their chance before the old bill had turned up, we walked down to the ground but at the turnstiles we were told there was no way that we were going to be allowed into the game. The stewards and security men locked the gates and refused to let us in. That left only one thing to do and that was to burst through the couple of Old Bill with us and sort out the mouthy mob of West Ham that had followed us down from the pub. We steamed straight into them and again they scattered. Normal West Ham fans and passersby looked on in amazement. They didn't have a clue who we were and what this was all about.

In the end we cleared the street and the place was deserted. We got back on the train with our job done, well pleased with ourselves. A few West Ham drove past us in cars and told us to get off at Mile End station. As we pulled in at Mile End the doors opened and there on the platform were 25 of West Ham's finest. We steamed straight out and straight into them and after a few punches they were on their toes and up the stairs and out of the station. We ended up going back to 'Shakes' pub in Victoria in a brilliant mood.

It turned out a good night for us and we saw it as a victory over the very unhappy Hammers. But there again they may have seen it different because as you know those marsh men don't like the taste of their own medicine.

CHAPTER EIGHT

WE ALL HATE LEEDS? WELL, NOT JUST LEEDS

Chelsea and Leeds have hated one another with a passion since we beat them in the 1970 F.A. Cup final. The teams drew 2-2 at Wembley and then we beat them 2-1 in the replay at Old Trafford. They hate us for beating them and we hate them for hating us. You'd only understand if you were a football fan. Leeds has a good firm called 'The Leeds Service Crew' and over the years have done the business all over the country.

They're one of the teams that do actually travel and love them or hate them, they turn up and they will oblige. They never duck out of a row. They've been to Millwall, West Ham, Man Utd and Chelsea in big numbers and put on a show.

For a League game up, there we met early at Kings Cross. It was that early that all the Brasses, Trannies, Drunks, Junkies and Pimps were still out on the streets. I'd been out on the piss and clubbing all night so I came straight from having a serious drinking session to meet the lads so I hadn't had a wink of sleep. It's only 6.00 a.m. and there's already a good 100 strong Chelsea mob waiting to board the first train north, many with their plastic shopping bags full of booze and a 'Sun' newspaper crumpled under their arm. I waited for the second train and journeyed up with Giles, Skitzy, and Ian from Lewisham, Smithy, Cooper and Doddy.

The student rail cards and Persil vouchers were doing overtime today. I've never seen so many students aged 25 and over. The plan was to meet up with the rest of the Chelsea firms in Wakefield as we had arranged a meet with their Service Crew away from Leeds City Centre. On the way up, we had a few games of cards and a puff. The plan was a Chelsea fan that lived in Wakefield was opening the doors of his pub early so we could have a drink and see how the day panned out before going off to the game. Leeds was supposedly meeting in a pub just up the road from us and would get in touch when they were ready for some action.

After a couple of hours of boredom and keeping a rumbling stomach in check (I hadn't eaten for nearly 24 hours and was fed up with drinking), me and Ian decided to have a scout about and maybe get some grub. We ended up sitting in the waiting room of the station where there was a small refreshment bar, drinking coffee and having a puff. After about 10 minutes, a train pulled in and about 60 fellas got off and nervously had a look around. "Here we go," I said to Ian, "these cunts aint Chelsea."

The two at the front spotted us and bowled over, all flash and cocky. "You two cockneys?" We looked at one another. I don't know if the weed had taken effect or we just couldn't be bothered to answer such a predictable and stupid question, but before we could decide on a suitable answer, over their shoulders I could see a 300 strong Chelsea mob that had just left the pub heading in our direction. "If I was you mate I'd fuck off a bit lively because you're just about to get fucked." Before he could say "is that right?" his mate looked around. He suddenly stopped bouncing on the spot and unclenched his fist. He tapped his mate "where's ya fucking firm Chelsea?" he growled, ignoring his mate tapping his arm. "Mate, do ya self a favour and fuck off," I said, and with that I just lost it and gave these two mugs a slap. Our lot swarmed through the doors of the station and within seconds the Leeds (not very reliable) Service Crew was off. The ones we caught got well smashed and they weren't so flash now.

We caught the train into Leeds but all that was waiting for us was none of their firm, but lines and lines of police. Nothing happened before or during the game and afterwards we set off on the long walk back to the station. We had a massive mob and Leeds just couldn't compete with us. There was the odd scuffle and we chased the odd little group of Leeds up side roads but there was nothing to write home about, has we sat on the train back to London, well fucked after a long day, talk got around to Man Utd, who had pulled one of our lads outside Euston that morning and had told him that if any Chelsea fancied a row that evening then a United firm would be stopping off in Peterborough after their match in London. They had a few boys that lived in the area, plus a few Mancs from up North were supposedly stopping off with them to have booze.

About 40 of us were up for it and tried to coax the rest of the train to join us. "They won't be there" was the reaction from almost everyone on the train. "Who said they're going to be there?" someone asked. "Steve Rutland reckons he's spoken to a couple of the Cockney Reds this morning." "Don't believe that lying cunt, he's full of shit," someone said and all the carriage laughed and nodded in agreement.

We pulled into Peterborough still trying to talk the rest of the train into getting off and joining us. "You're wasting your time," someone shouted as the train pulled off to London leaving us standing on the platform. Right outside the station was a big, old-fashioned pub called, yes you've guessed it, 'The Railway Arms'. A big homemade poster held on by cello tape was stuck to the front doors. "DISCO TONITE" it read. We opened the doors and sure enough, there was a DJ with sounds blasting out of the speakers, in the corner. "Now, let's get things in order," I'm thinking to myself. "Beer, food, puff, minge." D.J. Nicey done his best by keeping everyone off the dance floor and playing crap music and time just flew as the barman rang the bell for last orders. That was it for a Saturday night disco at the Railway Arms. It couldn't get any less exciting. No birds, no action, no punch-ups and no Man Utd. How fucking boring. Nicey thanked everyone for coming and told everyone he'd see them again and to blah blah blah have a safe journey home. Fucking hell, he was one boring cunt. We'd been told by one of the barmaids that there were two nightclubs in the town and that we might get in, if we were well behaved. The first one we came to the bouncers saw us coming and locked the doors. We walked on to the other one and the place looked like it was in darkness. They'd obviously heard we were in town so it was "lock up ya daughters." time, so there was nowhere left to go, only the cold dark waiting room on the train station if that wasn't locked up, and the long wait for the first train back to London in the morning.

I hadn't been to bed now for nearly 48 hours. A local pointed us in the direction of a fish and chip shop that might still be open. A few of the young lot eager to get there before us set off a bit lively. About 100 yards ahead of us we could see shadows and figures shouting and running about in the semi-darkness. Then the sound of glass can be heard smashing and a couple of our youngsters come running back, shouting that they've found the Mancs. The rest of them are fighting about 30 United outside the chip shop. Lee is the first one in from our lot and chins a geezer. Giles whacks another geezer and the blokes out cold, but United are game and stand their ground, and trade punches. A couple of them smash the bottles of drink they've just got from the fish shop and wave them around as weapons. That's it. Out come the blades and now they were going to get seriously hurt if they didn't back off. With a flash of the steel that was the signal for them to run and we cleared them off the streets. A couple of them were slashed and one stabbed and they were left where they fell. As we were walking away, job done the old bill arrived with two of the Mancs, in tow, who proceeded to point people out. We'd been a bit too clever, was clued up, and had already started swapping tops and jackets with each other just to confuse the issue of identification. The old bill took two of ours away as the Mancs stood their sniggering. The grassing no good cunts. The ones in our firm involved in the slashing managed to hide up until the 5.00 a.m. train back to London.

Terry Kent, one of those arrested, was taken to court and got a 3-year prison sentence. It could have been worse for a lot more of us as one of the Mancs was in hospital in a coma for a month but when he came around, he had memory loss. For all the pressure Terry, was under he never grassed on any of the firm? Now that's what you call a loyal mate.

That incident played on my mind for various reasons, which I can't and won't go into. For a few seasons I used to pick what games, I went to and when my own children were young, I used to take them along to games.

The next bit of bother I got into was when we played Barnet in an F.A. Cup game. Me, Skin and me Glasgow Rangers mate were on our way back home after the game. We stopped off at Finsbury Park on the tube where we changed trains to a British Rail over ground to Enfield. We'd missed our connection so we came back outside the station and decided to have a couple of pints until our next train. We went into the 'George Robey' pub but as soon as we walked inside you could sense a strange atmosphere. We carried on drinking as normal as a group of blokes at the bar kept looking over at us. "That cunt's getting on my nerves" said Skin as one of them kept on screwing. "If you want Skin," I said, I'll go over and knock him out."

"No Bully leave it," said Skin and walked over to the bloke and caught him with a peach of a punch, and put him straight on his arse! It was a good shot and then it just went just like one of them old cowboy films with chairs, glasses, and bottles and bodies flying through the air and at one stage, we were being done. Four of them had been badly cut and my hands were cut to ribbons from the broken glass but we some how managed to hold off about 30 of them off and when it calmed down a bit we fucked off a bit lively.

We went upstairs to the platform to get the last train, and there were helicopters up in the air, police sirens going, blue lights flashing, and then the police appeared and collared us. We were taken to Islington nick, which is in Tolpuddle Street where our clothes were removed and we were put in white forensic suits. We were then all charged with G.B.H and after about 18 hours, were released. Then a few weeks later all charges were dropped. The governor of the pub told the same story to the police as I had. All C.C.T.V. footage had been wiped off and there was no evidence to convict us. The governor also spoke to the Barnet fans involved and really he done a great job in smoothing it all over.

When we were initially arrested, we were handcuffed in the back of a police car and we driven past the 'George Robey' pub where there was ambulances and police cars parked outside. It was like a scene from the T.V. show, 'Casualty' with the blue lights flashing and bodies being wheeled out on stretchers. "Do you know anything about that?" asked the copper driving. "No," I replied. "You should do," said the copper, "they're your victims."

The same season as this Barnet game, Chelsea went all the way to the F.A. Cup final at Wembley against Man Utd. After playing Barnet in the third round at Stamford Bridge, which the game ended in a 0-0 draw and they were the home team because they had switched the tie because their ground was to small. We then played them again at the Bridge with us as the home side in the replay. This time we hammered them 4-0. Carl Hoddle, our player manager, Glen's brother, was in the Barnet line up. The next round saw us draw Sheffield Wednesday at home which we drew 1-1. The replay saw us win 3-1 at Hillsborough.

The fifth round we won 2-1 at Oxford Utd and in the sixth round, we beat Wolves 1-0 at Stamford Bridge. I remember that game well as we had a massive firm waiting for the Wolves Subway Army who failed to show. In the semis held at Wembley for some reason or other we beat Luton 2-0 and the biggest cheer of the day was for the Blues old favourite, Kerry Dixon, who was plying his trade at Luton.

In the final that year, we played Man Utd and lost 4-0. It could have been so so different if Gavin Peacocks shot had of gone in instead of hitting the crossbar. Before the game, we had probably one of the biggest mobs I've ever seen at football. Our mob met at the 'Lily Langtree' pub just off Kilburn High Road. United were drinking in the 'Black Lion' or some coloured Lion, in Kilburn High Road. We had no Old Bill with us as the shout went up that we were on the march to find Uniteds firm. The mob was massive with a fair few boys down from Glasgow Rangers. We also had a few Dutch, Germans, and Belgiums mingling in with the firm. They were all friends of friends so there was no bother. We made our way across a housing estate and through a children's' play area. We snaked through side streets and then out onto Kilburn High Road. As I looked back, I had a sense of pride at the size of the mob. It was fucking huge. That's the only way I can describe it. I'd never seen a firm like it. We marched down the centre of the road stopping the traffic in both directions. A couple of Irish pubs were attacked and the shout went up from the front that United were just up ahead, and then it happened. The riot Old Bill, dressed in black boiler suits, with batons at the ready appeared and spoilt the fun. They were over everyone like a rash. If we had of got to United we would have slaughtered them. We had a mad, mad firm there.

Afterwards it was going off all over the place and lots of United's firm got well smashed.

The next time we met them at Wembley was in a Charity Shield game. A few of the Chelsea firm was meeting in a pub early, just off Great Portland Street, but the governor was a Celtic fan so quite a lot of our boys, what with the Ranger allegiance refused to drink there. The main meet was to be 'The North London Tavern' over in Kilburn. United were supposedly meeting just up the road in another boozer. When we arrived most of the boys were sunning themselves outside the pub. It was a beautiful summer's day and it aint too often you can sit topless outside a pub in the football season. In no time the pub was packed, the beer was flowing, and the toilets were just as packed with some of the boys having their daily intake of the old marching powder. We sat outside having a spliff and chatting to faces, we hadn't seen for ages, when three Old Bill riot vans pulled up across the road. Out got the police cameraman and set all his gear up. Then a mob of 200 Man Utd turned up. Our pub emptied and we fanned out across the road. The old bill sprung into action and politely asked us to return to the pub. We walked straight through them and towards the United firm, who by now had stopped. One of their boys, thinking the rest of the firm was behind him, got to within 50 yards of us, he then looked around and realized he was on his own, and legged it up a side road. The old bill quickly sealed off the road, held them back, and cleared us back towards the pub with dogs. We tried unsuccessfully to go at them from the side but again the old bill had it sussed and pushed us back.

Up at Wembley we just took the piss. Any Manc that looked like one of their boys got it. Afterwards we all met back up at Harlsden and it was a brilliant turn out. But I had other things on my mind and her name was Maxine, but that's another story! I didn't rate United then but over the last few years, they've got their act together and they're now as good as they were in the 70s.

CHAPTER NINE

THE ZULUS

Birmingham City's Zulu Warriors are one of the country's main football firms. They'd be in most hooligans' top six. They've been doing it for years, both at home and away. Their main rivals are Aston Villa and Wolves, and over the years, they've had some right battles with their Midlands neighbours. Chelsea and Birmingham have had their rows over the years and I'd give it honours just about even in the battles we've had with them. They've never really come to Chelsea in force but we've always gone up there and put on a show.

A few seasons back our firm were at Aston Villa and after the game a few of our boys were passing through the Bull Ring shopping centre when they came across a few of the Zulus. A fight started and one of their black faces was slashed down the face and neck and nearly had his ear taken off. In another incident after our F.A. Cup semi final against Man Utd at Villa Park, about 50 of our younger lot had a row with a few of the Zulus' top black boys that ran the doors in Birmingham City Centre. Apparently, our young lot smashed them up and down the road and turned them right over, so there's been a bit of history and bad feeling bubbling away there.

One Saturday Birmingham was away to Crystal Palace and we were at home to Southampton or Coventry or someone. After most home games, a lot of our boys would go back over to Victoria and drink in a little pub just around the corner from the station. One of our lads was walking across the concourse on Victoria Station on his way to the pub when he came across what he recognized as a bit of a football firm. Being nosey, he casually strolled over and asked who they were and what they were up to. At first, they thought he was a copper and didn't really want to say too much. He'd clocked their accents and knew they were Brummies. He explained to them that he was on his way to meet up with the rest of the Chelsea firm and told them where we'd be if they fancied a row. Our boy, on arrived at our meet, excitedly told the packed pub that Birmingham were in town and they were up for a row. Two of our lot set off to find the pub the Zulus were drinking in and after looking in a few pubs they eventually found them. One of their boys, on seeing our two walk in the pub, strolled over and explained that they were not ready yet as they were waiting for the rest of their firm to turn up. For some reason our two boys, who are not known for their compassion and understanding, agreed that we'd give the Zulus more time to get their act together, and returned to the pub where there was now 30 to 40 Chelsea waiting for the signal to move.

After half an hour, one of our young lot was dispatched off to the Brummie pub just to see what was happening. If the boot was on the other foot and it was Chelsea up in Birmingham and we turned around and said we weren't quite ready, then I'm sure the Zulus would have seen this as an opportunity to attack. There's absolutely no way that Birmingham would let another firm drink in their city centre and get away with it. Our scout reported back that there was a good 50 Brummies in the pub now so the decision was made to launch an attack. A few of our young lot run up ahead and put the windows in with bricks and bit and pieces they'd just pulled from a builders' skip. The Brummies near to the windows and doors immediately backed off. The rest of the boys forced their way into the pub and the Brummies scattered. A few stood and fought but they were soon overpowered.

With the job done, our boys backed out of the pub but a few of the Brummies must have seen this as a Chelsea retreat, and followed us out of the pub. We turned and steamed straight back into them and a few of them took a kicking. Police sirens soon filled the air and it was time for us to vanish. It was good while it lasted and there were no arrests on our side. I don't know if any of the Brummies got nicked but we did bump into them when we played them in the Cup in the '04-'05 season.

We drew Birmingham in the F.A. Cup down at The Bridge and before the game a mob of their mainly black boys came out of Fulham Broadway at about 2 45 p.m. They were surrounded by old bill and didn't look up to much. Afterwards they nearly came unstuck out on the Fulham Road where they were backed up against a wall and the intervention of the old bill was the only thing that saved them. The old bill baton charged our mob up the various side roads running off the Fulham Road, and allowed Birmingham's mob to walk, unescorted, towards Fulham Broadway station. They took a few liberties, and beat up a lone Chelsea fan, and gave it the biggan when only a few minutes before they'd been pinned up against a wall shitting themselves. The old bill caught up with them outside one of the pubs at the Broadway and surrounded them before they came to any harm. I looked at them and thought to myself, "if that's what the Zulu warriors have come to then boys, your days are numbered. You're finished as a firm."

Another time when a small group of us took on another firm with not very big numbers was when we played Millwall in a night game at 'The Bridge.' Don't get me wrong, I'm not saying Millwall can't pull a big firm and aint got the numbers, but on this particular night the row was between a few of ours and a handful of theirs. Me, Tony C. and Giles and two others came out of the West stand just as the game was finishing. A mob of 200 Millwall came towards us from the other side of the ground and the two fellas who'd joined us earlier, on seeing the Millwall mob, decided it wasn't for them and said they no longer wanted to be part of this daft plan. The old bill got in between the Millwall firm, us before it went mental, and the situation was defused. Fuck me I've done some daft things at football but that one tops it all.

Liverpool were another team that came to Chelsea in the Cup when we beat them 4-2, and there was running battles with little mobs of Scousers' all over the place. We didn't give a fuck how many of them there was. After the game we steamed into them on the escalators at Euston and ran them everywhere. Outside in Euston Square, a couple of Scousers pulled blades but we didn't care and just went into them and they soon fucked off. Liverpool are one mob I don't rate at all. To me they've just got a big group of singers. They're more like a street gang than a football mob, and fucking scruffy, they must be one of the fucking scruffiest firms I've ever come across. How have they got the fucking cheek to say they were the originators of the Casual look?

We fucked them in the semi finals at Old Trafford a couple of seasons ago when we took a 400 strong mob up there, but they didn't want to come out and play. Perhaps they were too busy trawling the charity shops of Manchester for their fashion accessories. Hold up. Weren't they the cunts that had the big curly perms and the silly little tashes? I don't remember us having that look in London, nor the Shell suits. I didn't see that look take off in London either. "Calm down, calm down."

CHAPTER TEN

"THE YIDS"

My recollections of clashes with Tottenham are that I've never ever been done by them. It's as simple as that. I'm not saying they haven't got a good firm, because they have. Chelsea and Tottenham have hated one another since the 1967 Cup final when they beat us 2-1. Since that day, there's been plenty of bad blood between the two mobs and plenty of blood spilled. Talk to any Arsenal fan and they'll tell you their main rivals, and the team they hate the most are their North London neighbours, Spurs. Ask most Spurs fans who they hate the most and I bet a fair few of them will say Chelsea, even more so since the Abramovitch revolution.

We played Spurs a few seasons back in a night game at the Bridge and I'll be totally honest and say Spurs took the piss that night. For the previous few seasons, their mob had failed to show. Personally, I think it was after they got smashed by our lot at The Argyle pub in Central London. A black day in the history of the Yid Army.

At this particular game we played them at Stamford Bridge, they came over early doors and drank in a pub, which was quickly surrounded by Old Bill, and no one was allowed within a hundred yards of the pub. Tottenhams' mob claims they had had a result because they were drinking in a pub in the Kings Road. Surely, a result is when you have a fight with a rival firm and smash them or run them. Ordering a bottle of Becks and standing at the bar trying to look hard is hardly having a result. Knowing that you are drinking in a comfort zone with lines of old bill covering your arses and protecting you from attack, that's a result is it.

In the night game at our place, as I said, they did do well. Our organization that night went to pot. We had three or four small mobs of 40 to 50 split in different locations. Spurs came early, were well organized and took us by surprise. This time they came to fight and fight they did, and they did well before and after the game. They had a 300 strong mob standing on the main forecourt after the game and looked impressive. We just couldn't get our act together. Our firm around this time was getting lazy and complacent. We thought we could take anyone on, sometimes-just 20 handed, and have a result. We'd done it against so many teams and got away with it.

Fighting at football at times is like playing poker. It's all about front and bluff and our firm have plenty of that. In addition, it does help to have some serious madmen and some game fuckers, and we have both. We've pulled some big firms together yet there have been other times when we've gone somewhere twenty handed. Don't get me wrong. We've had the best, pound for pound; twenty probably in the country, but it was only a matter of time before we came unstuck. We had the warning a few years back when Tony C. led twenty of us into Leicester and took on their Baby Squad. I've said to Giles and Tony C. and The Twins "We can't carry on like this" and that Spurs game at home proved this. I heard Spurs had a big mob that met on the 'Tattershall Castle' boat, which is moored on the Thames. They also had a mob that got off at Wandsworth British Rail station and walked down via Wandsworth Bridge. They planned it perfectly. To me I didn't think the 'Yids' had their top firm out that night but on the day, they were too good for us. We clashed with them just before the game on the bridge down the Kings Road. Spurs had been drinking in 'Reilly's' bar near The Worlds End. Loads of us had the hump about that and moral was low. Anyway, after that disastrous night, we didn't have to wait long before we played Spurs again but this time it was over at their place.

Two days before the game a couple of us went over to Tottenham and had a scout about. We had a look at a couple of pubs and settled on one as a good place to meet. On the day of the game, there was two meets. We met in a pub in Bethnal Green at 7.30 a.m. and the other meet was in South London where two 52 seater coaches had been booked to ferry the other part of our firm across London to Ponders End station where they'd leave the coaches and come into Tottenham by train from a direction the police and the Yids wouldn't suspect. In the end, three coaches went straight to the pub where, on their arrival, there was already a good 200 strong Chelsea firm. By midday the place was packed with about 350 – 400 serious, Chelsea faces. There was people there I hadn't seen for years. This was more like it. The old bill had obviously done their homework and was outside the pub in huge numbers. The Yids were nowhere to be seen and we'd not heard a peek from them, on the mobiles, since we'd arrived, but a few of the lads on the coaches said they drove past one of Tottenham's pub and some of their firm were drinking outside and when they saw the coaches go by with our boys looking at them from the windows, their jaws nearly hit the floor. Now that was taking the piss. If the Yids had of turned up where we were drinking they would have got mullered as this was a magnificent Chelsea firm.

About one o'clock the old bill came in the pub and one by one searched everyone. Then it was names and addresses and a photograph and a body search. There must have been 200 Old Bill in and around the pub. Only about 30 of us had tickets for the game. Then it was time for the old bill to move us. The pub we were in was in the Northumberland Park part of Tottenham, which is just behind the Park Lane end of the ground. As we left the pub under a huge police escort, a mob of Tottenham came out of the flats from a run down council estate and we just stormed across the road and ran them. A couple of theirs were knocked down in the rush but were rescued by the old bill before they got seriously hurt. As the old bill moved us slowly towards the ground, a mob of Tottenham came in front of us and spread themselves out across the road. We just kept walking towards them with the old bill holding us back. They backpedaled all the way to the Park Lane. It was all their main boys but we'd have been too much for them and they knew it. We were held in the street outside the ground surrounded by old bill. I was standing next to a copper and his radio burst into life. Whoever was talking on the other end described what had been left behind in the pub we'd just left. Basically the policemen's' radio blurted out that marijuana, cocaine, meat cleavers, flick knives, coshes, hammers, axes, ammonia and C.S. gas canisters had all been found in the pub.

It was now three o'clock and the boys started to get a bit restless. Further, up the road a large mob of Tottenham was making themselves busy so we decided to walk towards them. Now the two firms were only 50 yards apart. We pushed forward through the old bill and the majority of the Spurs firm backed off into Tottenham High Road. More police on horse back arrived and forced us back.

We were going nowhere. The police split us into three different groups and one by one; they pulled us out and handcuffed us with those plastic ties they use when they've run out of metal handcuffs it was a sort of mass nicking on the cheap! We were then videod and put on board a police coach. We were driven to Islington police station with a police helicopter hovering and following us overhead. We had about 10 police outriders on motorbikes escorting us who went in front to see us straight through any red traffic lights. It was utter madness. How much did this operation cost? This was more like a terrorist operation not the transportation of a group of football fans.

We finally arrived at Islington Police station at 5.15 p.m. and they held us outside for another two and a half hours because, in their words, we might well go back over to the Tottenham area and finish what we had started. Eventually the coaches pulled away from the police station and we drove around London for a bit then we stopped at various underground stations where the bus was emptied of its human cargo. At each stop, six people were allowed to leave the coach, then it was off to another stop, and then another six were allowed to leave and then so on until the coach was empty.

At Islington police station, all those on the coaches were charged with Section 60s, which while processing everyone they ran out of the paper work. These Section 60 orders meant that if you were seen in the vicinity of where you had just been arrested within an allocated time then you could be arrested instantly and charged with something else. All it really is is a warning to fuck off out of it or go away and stay away. It's purely a warning and they say it doesn't go on record. Yea right! All that paperwork and nothing's done with it pull the other one.

I was dropped off near Victoria Station and people who lived in South London were dropped off at Euston or Kings Cross. The old bill knew what we were capable of going back and doing, and they weren't taking any chances. The coppers that were sitting down with us as the coach drove around London were to be honest all right. The decision to carry out this operation must have been taken from very high up because it was a high security, high budget carry on.

I went home that night and thought we'd done well. The feed back from some of my Spurs mates was zilch, zero, nothing. They knew we'd turned up over there and done the bizzo. It was like in their book we hadn't even showed up. It was like the game hadn't even been played. It was never mentioned. The thing is, going to watch a game at Tottenham, as an away fan is almost impossible, as you can't get a match ticket, the tickets for away fans are like gold dust the allocation is very small and most go to season ticket holders.

Last season at our place they turned up a couple of hundred strong and we attacked them down near the cemetery on Fulham Road. We were driven back by the riot old bill, with gas and batons at the ready. They then came onto the forecourt and we were waiting for them. "Yid Army, Yid Army," they were confidently chanting. That was until they saw us and then they shut right up. If it wasn't for the old bill, we would have killed them and they know it.

During and after the game the old bill surrounded the pub our firm was in and blocked off all the side roads leading from the Fulham Road. The Yids were escorted down the underground, and put on a train and whisked away, a victory to the old bill.

I do rate Spurs but they cannot for some reason give credit when credit is due. As a firm, I'd put them in my top six. My run-ins with

Tottenham go back a long way. A few seasons ago me and me mate Scotcher had two tickets for a game over at White Hart Lane. I told him it was dodgy for me and him to go over there on our own as I was well known over there, and I told him that I normally went over with the firm. "Don't worry, he said, let's just go over there and watch the football, have a few beers and keep out of trouble, and keep our heads down"

I picked him up in me van, parked me van around at me mum's in Edmonton and walked down towards the ground. As we came past a couple of the Tottenham pubs I could see their firm drinking in there and a few of their boys were hanging about outside. I swerved them and totally ignored them. As we got nearer to the ground, a big mob of Spurs came down the road and head the same way as us. I don't like the look of this and whisper to Scotcher that "Chelsea must be about," As we get outside the West Stand entrance there's a mob of Chelsea standing outside 'Rudolph's Bar.' My good mates, Prikey and John Carling are there with a good little firm. Someone says that Tottenham's firm are standing outside the Paxton Road entrance and our lot set off to find them. Scotcher and me follow behind and he's not too sure, what's going on. "Bully?" he asks, "I thought we were only here to watch the football." I don't answer his question and turn the corner into the Paxton Road, where there are lines of old bill stopping the Chelsea fans from going any further. Scotcher doesn't look like a football thug so we were allowed straight through. Only me Scotcher, Cooper, Pike and Beast get through out of that group of Chelsea fans. We carried on walking up towards the ground and a firm of Spurs came up behind us. A few of them knew my name. "Bully, Bully, come on, where's ya firm?" A few of them hissed. They started spitting and bouncing about in the road and calling us mugs. "What do you want to do, there's only five of us?" I said and that was it; I'd heard enough and flew straight into them. My initial attack shocked them and I backed them off. Fists then came at my head from every direction and I managed to get one geezer down and was kicking the fuck out of him. Every time a fist connected with my head, I kicked this cunt on the floor even harder. I then had him by the hair, was pulling his big jumbo ears off, and was kneeing him in the bollocks. "Tell ya mates to back off, I told him, or I'll break ya fucking neck." I let the bloke stand up and he was wobbling all over the place. I cracked him on the jaw to finish him off and about five of them swarmed all over me. I fought back and backed them off. "Come on Chelsea," said one mouthy Yid. As I stood there covered, in blood, the old bill came along and everyone dispersed, except of cause me. I was thrown into the ground by the old Bill and after a while found my seat. No one sitting near me said a word. My clothes were ripped and I was covered in blood. I had the right hump. My best Lacoste shirt and cardigan was ripped to shreds. Outside after the game I was well pissed off and just fucked off and picked my van up from my mum's and shot off home. I wasn't in a very good mood.

Tottenham say our darkest day was when we played them in 1975 and they beat us 2-0 in a First Division game at White Hart Lane, which in reality sent us down. We needed to beat Spurs and beat Sheffield United at home to have any chance of staying up. We drew 1-1 with Sheffield United so we ended up being relegated with Carlisle, and Luton and Spurs also in the relegation battle stayed up.

At the Spurs game, which saw a crowd of nearing fifty two thousand packed into the ground, there was fighting all round the place. The few Chelsea fans that had found their way into the Park Lane were attacked and ran onto the pitch. The ones in the Paxton Road were out numbered and faced wave after wave of Spurs attacks. Some Chelsea went onto the pitch to get away. Spurs fans joined them and the fighting carried on on the pitch. The bulk of the Chelsea firm that day was locked outside unable to get in. It may well have been a different story if our firm had been in the ground and I bet the Spurs firm wouldn't have had it all their own way.

Another row we had with Spurs was when we were on our way back from playing Birmingham City. We'd had a good day out in Birmingham and had run their firm ragged all day long after Birmingham had called it on at Solihull. We had 250 of us on a train up from Marylebone to Snow Hill in Birmingham. We got up there by 10.30 in the morning, with not a copper in sight yet the Zulus couldn't get a firm organized or get from one part of Birmingham to another. They were embarrassing that day and they knew we were too much for them. Two of Birmingham's boys came into the pub we were drinking in and asked if we had a younger mob. "No mate," one of our boys said, we're all together and we're Chelsea." "We can't match this," said the Brummies and fucked off. They were lucky to get out in one piece. It was only because they knew Fat Pat that they were allowed to leave in one piece.

After the game 16 of us caught the early, train back to London and just by sheer coincidence 15 Spurs fans got on at Reading station, where if I remember rightly, they were on their way back from a day out at Newbury races. They got on board the train and it kicked off straight away. The Twin chinned two of them and received a black eye back for his efforts. I was fighting with one of them in the corridor and because of the limited space we couldn't really get into one another. They had a couple of big, black geezers with them who didn't really want to get to the front of their mob and perform they looked like they'd bottled it a bit. The fight went on from Reading station to Slough station. At Slough, the Spurs Boys seemed to shuffle along the corridor and backed off the train doors opened for a while and then they shut. We were all thinking "this is it; it's going to go all the way to Marylebone station." We were rubbing our hands together. We couldn't wait, but unbeknown to us the police have got on at Slough further along the platform and had lead the Spurs firm off the train along and out through the carriage next to the driver's door. The first we realised that they were off the train was when the doors of the train shut and the train pulled out of the station and the Spurs mob were walking along the platform shouting abuse and giving us the wankers' sign. If only they'd used that amount of energy fighting us, they might have done a bit better. We'd called up Skinhead John and Panther and two mini buses full of Chelsea to meet us at Marylebone thinking that the Yid mob would be on the train all the way back into London. We had to phone them back and tell them the bad news that the old bill had rescued them at Slough.

Again, Swainy and his Spurs mates never acknowledged what we done that day. It's as if the incident never happened. As I say, I rate Tottenham as a firm more so than their North London neighbours, Arsenal. But they love to bury their heads in the sand when they get done, West ham are another firm like that.

We've had so many run ins with the Gooners over the years and hailing from North London, just a stones throw from Highbury, I know loads of their chaps. One game against them that sticks in my mind was when we played them in a friendly at The Bridge in 1982. They were then in the old First Division and we were in the Second Division. Arsenal's firm them days were calling themselves 'The Herd' and by all accounts, they rated themselves. This friendly game was going to be far from friendly. We hadn't played Arsenal for three or four years and had been mixing it with the likes of Luton, Wrexham, Bristol City and Grimsby. Now it was a chance to prove that we hadn't lost our touch with the so-called big boys. I knew John Stephens one of their main faces and along with Denton, were two of

I love it on the coast. One day I shall retire down by the sea

The lads on the trip to Milan

(*Facing page*) Victoria with some admirers

On holiday in the sun. Chelsea v Majorca, Semi-final. ECWCP

I did hear that Barcelona were after the geezer in the keeper's jersey

The chaps on the piss. Marriner looks his usual happy self

Outside the home of football

Me and Martin King

Me and Cooper at our H.Q. in the "La Reserve" in Fulham. "Come in if you dare"

Me and my daughter Alexandra

Me and Cooper out in Milan, in the wrong end

The Firm in Stockholm 99

Me, Lee, Stuart Glass, Del-boy and Warren Glass drinking over in Islington

Off to Ian Twin's wedding with Ian Lewisham

The usual suspects

(*Facing page*) Don't I look happy?

(*Next two pages*)
"Come on, who's round is it? Don't fuck about Matty, get ya money out

Napoli. My Italian hosts

Napoli. The police came under attack

Napoli. The away support is fenced in at the front and are under attack

Outside the Napoli Stadium. This feels like home

Arsenal's boys that ran the show over there. I knew that if Arsenal turned up then those two would be at the front. The thing was that neither Denton nor Stephens would tell me what Arsenal's plans were. The pub I drank at in Islington was used by a few of the Arsenal faces so I listened into a few of the conversations and gleamed a bit of inside information.

On the day of the game, which was in midweek, we started meeting up at Fulham Broadway at about 2.00 p.m. By 4.00 p.m. The Swan pub had a 200 strong Chelsea mob in there. I spoke to Micky Nagle, Stephen's cousin, the night before the game but he was giving nothing away. He did say though that 'The Herd' was coming and had plans to meet up on our territory. The only thing with Arsenal's firm is they have a history of turning up late and trying to surprise you or even worse not turning up at all. They've never been one of them teams that come over early and come looking for it. Nor do they get in a pub near to the ground early, get surrounded by the old bill and see that as a result. They do at least come for a row and not a drink.

By six o'clock, I'd had enough of swigging bottles of beer and I was bored and restless. I wanted to see some action so me, Cooper and Steve Rutland who, like me knew a few of Arsenals main faces, went and had a scout about. To our surprise, the streets around the ground were deserted. Hot dog, sellers and programme sellers were standing around scratching their nuts with literally no one to serve. We walked past a few of the pubs down near the ground and it was evident that they were packed out with boys who, if it came to it, would be out on the streets if and when the Gooners turned up. It seemed we had a firm in every pub. If they came out of Fulham Broadway then The Swan would have them covered. If they came from the Kings Road then The Brittania and The Palmerston could cover that. If they came from Sloane Square then The Gunter and The Black Bull had that covered and The Mulsters would cover any invasion from the Earls Court, Baron Court area.

By 7.30 p.m. they still hadn't shown and we were getting pretty pissed off. I told everyone that these cunts would definitely be making a show and if they didn't show then they would make me look a right soppy cunt. The game kicked off in lees then 15 minutes and a lot, of the Battersea boys had had enough of waiting for the Gooners. "Come on, this is fucking silly, them cunts aint coming," was the general consensus. I managed to talk about fifty of our boys into giving it another five minutes. From inside the ground we could hear a muffled down beat cheer as the teams came onto the pitch and the game, kicked off. The crowd was only just over eight thousand so there were lots of empty spaces on the terraces.

A lot of the boys holding back with me were from North London and had a bit of a point to prove. A few of the youngsters with me were originally followers of Arsenal but because of the lack of action over at Highbury, they had switched their allegiance to Chelsea. In them days, we had a far better firm. In the late 60s and throughout the 70s Arsenal had a top firm, probably the best in London. They had the likes of Johnny Hoy and Stan Jackson and George the Greek at the front of their mob. The North Bank Highbury was a fortress and not many teams ventured in there and tried to take it. In the 80s and early 90s, their firm fell into decline and it was only the likes of Smithy, Denton and Miller that kept it going.

At five past eight there, was some movement on the streets as the old bill appeared and looked a bit busy. Then I heard the war cry. "Arsenal, Arsenal, Arsenal, Arsenal." Now there was only about 25 of us and it was now our job to block their route into the ground. They came running over the bridge on the Fulham Road and turned right onto the forecourt at the Shed end. We spread out and moved towards them. The old bill had already lost control and didn't really have the manpower to deal with it. The two mobs clashed. They were about 80 handed but we stood and traded punches and kicks. One of their front men went down and they began to back off. We pushed forward and forced them back across the road. The old bill got their act together and swamped all over everyone and surrounded them as the fighting ended, as quickly as it had begun. They then marched the Arsenal firm down to the North stand and walking at the front was John Stephens. I put my hand up and waved at him and as I done this two coppers nabbed me and nicked me for threatening behaviour.

I was taken to Fulham police and put in a cell. Through my peephole in the door, I could see the names of those arrested. I'd given the police a statement and told them I was an Arsenal fan that had been split up from my mates. Mine was the next name to go up on the board. All in all there was 14 people arrested and charged, 13 from Chelsea and me from Arsenal. The only good thing was we were allowed out after the game and we caught the last orders at 'The Swan' pub at Fulham Broadway before the last train back to North London.

Those fucking Gooners weren't going to hear the last of this. I remember the look of fear on their faces as we chased them across the road and the smirks on their faces as I was arrested and led away. At least I was in a firm more famed for its fighting than for its running.

CHAPTER ELEVEN

CHELSEA IN EUROPE

The first time I ever got to see Chelsea play in Europe was against FK Austria Vienna. We drew the first leg at home in the Cup Winners Cup 0-0 so it didn't look too good for the away leg in Vienna.

We travelled from Gatwick and there was a big Chelsea firm at the airport the place was packed, Arsenal had not long played out there and they'd apparently come unstuck in a park near to the stadium. I think Fat Pat had phoned around all the Chelsea lads and rallied the troops for this trip out to Austria. It turned out we had no trouble in the park because we had one massive firm out there. We walked everywhere looking for their firm. After the game, there was a little bit of trouble in the city centre. We were all in a couple of bars and a firm of Austrians came out of the underground station and fired a couple of distress flares at one of the bars. Within seconds the packed bar emptied and they were chased off into the night.

The game ended in a 1-1 draw which put us through on the away goals rule. John Spencer got our goal and what a goal it was. He run near on the length of the field before slotting the ball into the net. Fuck me, it was some goal. That night we had a firm and a half and there wouldn't be many teams that could have lived with us. We'd stayed on the piss nearly all night and got all drunk and silly, but it was a good trip.

Milan was another good trip in the 'Champions League'. That was the game when Dennis Wise scored. Before the game their Ultras came around looking for us but we didn't bump into them. We took the Metro to the stadium and then we walked all around the ground with a huge mob. The stadium with its lights on, and the surrounding neighbourhood in darkness, made the stadium look like a space ship or a U.F.O., which had landed in the middle of nowhere. It's a strange sight and an awesome ground. Six of us went in the wrong section of the ground and then things started changing. We somehow had tickets in with the Italians. We'd bought a package of a flight and a match ticket. Nothing was said as we queued to get in, it was only when we found our seats that the crowd around us got a bit hostile. We started talking about Napoli (who the Northern Italians hate with a passion) and getting a bit loud. They were doing the throat cutting action and pulling make believe guns out of their coats and pointing them at us. Me and Cooper had Napoli badges on our jackets and that didn't go down too well. They really hate Napoli with a passion. Then Wisey scored and we just give it to them. We'd had a good drink and really gave it to everyone around us. They stood up and was shouting and swearing at us. They had the right hump.

At the end of the game we held back as the thousands of Chelsea fans at the other end of the ground celebrated the result. We let the Italians around us leave the stadium, not because we were worried but it gave us a bit more space to see what was going on. A few of them made a feeble effort to get into us but we stood firm and they didn't fancy mixing it with us.

For the game against Majorca I booked five days out there. It was the best game I've ever been to. You had everything, the sun, the sea, the booze the football. It was fucking paradise. It was the semi final of the Cup Winners Cup and there was no trouble and a great place to watch football. A little bit different to watching Chelsea in Paris, the so-called City of Love.

I'd finished work and me, John Bud and Barry Fields were having a drink in the pub and the draw came on for the next stage of the Champions' League. Chelsea were grouped with the Russians, CSKA Moscow, Porto, the Portuguese team which was another couple of days in the sun, and the French team, Paris St Germaine (PSG). This was a great draw and I could just imagine all them Stone Island Keyboard Warriors' fingers being, red hot doing overtime on their P.C.s posting messages on the hooligan web sites. The sad cunts. P.S.G. had already done battle with Arsenal and Glasgow Rangers in the previous years and by all accounts, both teams had held their own and had done well. In football terms P.S.G at home to Chelsea had all the makings of a serious row. We would need to take at least 200 good boys to do battle with 'The Boulogne Boys' as their mob was known. Now was the time to book my trip to France and I had to act quickly as these greedy travel companies double and sometimes treble their prices when there's a sniff of a football match in the air. They get so greedy and they know most die-hard football fans will pay almost anything to see their team. A normally £100 trip can, within hours of the draw, became a £400 trip. They just rip you off and they know it the smug bastards. The other alternative is to join the police and be posted to the football intelligence unit where you can go abroad for the football for nothing, all expenses paid. How bad is that? And you do fuck all while you're out there. Just take some photos or shoot some video footage of anyone aged between 16 and 75. What a cushy job! The only criteria are you have to be slightly overweight, have no personality and own a wax jacket. Why do them undercover coppers wear wax jackets at football? For fucks sake, you're at football not fox hunting. You look out of place; you stand out a mile with your naff haircuts and sticking out ears. Well, that's what happens with them helmets weighing down on them and pushing them out of place.

On the day of the game I left my home in Enfield at 3.00 am and drove over to Stuart Glass's house in West London. My daughter Victoria and her mate Kelly came with me and took the van back home for me. We left Stuart's at 5.00 p.m. and picked up our mate Ian and then headed to Dover in cars. This was a good firm, Steve, PJ, Stuart, Simon, Muzza, Pascalle Lee, Ian and Dell-boy were some of Chelsea's finest and a couple of them had been out to Paris before with Glasgow Rangers so we had some first hand information and experience of their firm. As I say, Arsenal had been there a few seasons before and quite a few of their boys were injured. But then again they were rowing with the French who were tooled up to the eyeballs. They had gas, baseball bats, knives, lumps of wood, shovels; supposedly the lot, but the French didn't have it all their own way with the Gooners. A good few of the Frogs were injured. The running battles went on for hours with Arsenal standing and running them and then the French coming back and running them. All the time the P.S.G. mob were doing ok the French riot police stood by and let it happen but as soon as Arsenal got the upper hand then the police would step in, crack a few English heads, fire a few CS canisters and clear the streets. Well, with Arsenal's mob they didn't only crack English heads, there would have been, amongst them. Irish,

Nigerians, Turks, Greeks, West Indians, Armenians, Kazakhs, Tamils, Azerbaijanis, Kurds and Pygmies in their multi cultural firm.

Before we crossed over to France we had to have an English breakfast. The usual double egg, bacon, sausage, bubble, black pudding, beans, tomatoes, tea, and toast. Why do we English have to have a full breakfast before we leave these shores? Do you think the French; have coffee and a croissant before they cross their borders? The sea was very rough on the crossing and I could feel my breakfast moving about, my stomach wasn't very happy. Dell-boy was worse as he didn't have very good sea legs. Once on the other side it was then a 3 hour, drive down to Paris. We were through passport control with no bother, and once in Paris we found the hotel we were all booked into for the night. We then dropped off our gear and set out to find the rest of the Chelsea boys. We had a few beers in a few different bars and slowly we began to all meet up. There was a strange atmosphere. No one was really knocking the booze back or putting huge amounts of gear up their noses. It was like we expected something big to happen, something out of the norm. A few faces looked a bit uneasy. It must have been that sixth sense thing?

By 5.15 p.m. we had a 200 strong firm. I wouldn't say it was one of our best as we had a lot of our youth with us. Don't get me wrong, they can row and are as game as fuck, but here, out in Paris, it was a whole new ball game for them and one day they will eventually replace the ageing Chelsea Head-Hunters, but for this moment in time they needed us and we needed them. We set off on the metro and came off at a Metro station, which looked just like a built up area of Paris. No old bill, and no French firm were awaiting our arrival. Someone pointed the way to the stadium and off we marched. A few stopped for a quick toot off of the backs of their hands and then we set off as one nice and tight and all together firm. Now the feeling was getting better. This was more like it. We had a bit of a spring in our step, more of a buzz, or maybe it was just the Charlie kicking in.

We were walking down a wide avenue with trees either side. A couple of our young spotters were 500 yards in front of us and a mobile phone rang. "Boys," said the voice on the other end, "their main bar is on the corner of the next block." We spread across the pavement and into the road and our firm looked huge. "Hold the line," said a voice at the front. "Steady boys, hold up, and don't run at them." The P.S.G. firm were now out on the street and coming towards us, bottles and glasses smashed as they now ran towards us. You could smell gas in the air. They were shouting and screaming as they ran towards us. "Walk, walk Chelsea." We walked calmly and purposefully towards them. Their mob grinds to a halt as now they're yards from us. Their front line is trying to turn away from us, not a good sign. Their hangers on at the back have already seen enough and are on their toes. A few of their front line go down as we steam into them, kicking and punching. Lots of individual fights are breaking out as the English get the upper hand. Leafy suburban Paris comes to a halt as the Chelsea mob run the French everywhere. They're going in all directions, in and out of cars, and swerving traffic that is moving. Many of them go up side streets and are away. 1-0 to the Chelsea boys. We re-group and march on. We know that's not the end of it and we know they'll be back. I looked around and our numbers had dwindled. We were down to about 120-150. The French old bill were now on the scene but stand back looking pretty in all their body armour and guns and gas and utility belts with the matching dangling handcuffs, it's all very Prada.

Then their firm re-appears. "Here we go boys, it's round two," someone shouts, and the two firms clash and it's toe to toe, but we're holding strong. C.S. gas fills the air and a roar goes up and we back them off. We make another charge and we've now got the French on the move and they have a look of fear and panic on their faces.

They disappear up a side street that looks like it leads directly to the stadium. Now we have a line of riot Old Bill in front of us fully armed and not looking best pleased. We've just run their boys, and we're now down to about 90 to 100 and to tell you the truth, although we've done well, it's not looking good. We've received a few injuries with cut heads and gas burns and we've no substitutes to bring on and replace the injured. This ain't football ya know. We're stopped from moving forward or going on by two lines of old bill. Then without warning, they roll an opened gas canister into our ranks. Clouds of gas rise up and a couple of the lads pull out swimming goggles from inside their coats. Others pull up the hoods of their tops and put hankies over their mouths. We move off and turn up another street and the stadium is just up ahead of us. We now numbered only about 60. I think a lot of our firm didn't mind taking on the P.S.G mob but not the French riot police, so they gave it the slip. A lot of our boys also thought that was it and the fighting was over but us die hard, hardcore 60 knew that it wasn't. Me, Pat, Stuart and Jock were buzzing and we wanted more. We should have taken what we'd done and had the result and just gone into the ground, but us Chelsea boys have a different mentality. We don't know when to call it a day. We'd proved ourselves but we felt we had to march on.

A park came up ahead and a 200 strong French firm faced us. We didn't give a fuck that they had the superior numbers and went straight into them. This took them by surprise and they backed off. They suddenly realized that we only had small numbers compared to them and began raining missiles down on us, lumps of rock, bricks, stones, bottles and glass landed in the middle of us and it split our mob into two. Their mob almost doubled in size in seconds as word got around that we were there. We were standing next to a bike park and used the bikes to make a barricade. Now it was really on top for us. We began to split up and get lost in amongst their mob but Pat and Stuart done well to keep some sort of front line and the French were a bit hesitatent to come into us. We rallied one more time, the adrenalin and the chang was mixing, together and racing through my veins. We stood and held firm and again we backed them off.

Then to the right of us came a mob down a dark side street their heads bobbing up and down as they came towards us. It looked like a scene from the London Marathon. "They're Chelsea," smiled Stuart. Was they fuck? This was another 300 strong mob of French. Now we were well fucked and surrounded. They showered us with missiles and we backed off now we were split as just seven of us stood facing this huge French mob. Some of them had taken their belts from their trousers and had wrapped the buckles around their fists. My face and eyes were burning from the effects of the C.S gas. I didn't want to be here. "Beam me up Scotty," I thought, if only. We try to pass a line of old bill that stood firm and wouldn't let us pass. The French firm knew they had us now, their old bill would allow them to do what they wanted and there was no fear of them being nicked. We squeezed up a side street and the Paris boys followed. A few more Chelsea appeared and there was fighting going on all around. One of the youth pulled from his jeans pocket his last gram of Charlie. Everyone's panicking and they're looking to me for wisdom and advice and a safe passage out of there. We do the chang and look for a way out. Behind us was a block of apartments and one of the residents had just let himself in through the front entrance and the door hadn't quite slammed shut. We squeezed through and in. The youth with me run up the stairs looking for a way to escape, I'm caught just inside the entrance in thc lobby. The P.S.G, firm have seen where we've gone and have kicked the door in and come steaming towards me. Next thing I know I've been gassed full in the face and as I put my hands up to wipe my eyes so that I can protect myself, I hear a bottle smash and then I feel a searing pain in my hand. I'm in a hell of a state. I run up one flight of stairs and bang on the first door I come to. I can hardly see. The door opens and the lady standing there looks at me and slams the door in my face. I run back down the stairs and I'm now starting to panic. My legs are buckling and I'm ready to pass out. I feel sick and my head is spinning. I can see I'm losing a lot of blood and then I realize I've been stabbed in the hand. Jock from Peterborough is the first person to find me, and then Ian from Middlesbrough turns up. The police come in and try to roughly pull me to my feet. Jock explains that I've been stabbed and then they've seen the blood and called for an ambulance. They pull me to my feet and they then realized that I'd been hurt badly.

It took the ambulance twenty minutes to get to me and as I was being put in the back, there was still a group of P.S.G. hanging around shouting insults. The old bill did nothing as usual and did nothing to move them on. The two paramedics in the ambulance were two gay guys who spoke good English. They told me that all the ambulance men and paramedics hated the P.S.G. supporters because every time they played there was trouble and there were always unnecessary injuries. Ian came with me to the hospital and I was seen straight away. I was bandaged up and given strong painkillers and placed on a ward. I was then taken for x rays and one of the nurses explained that I was going to be operated on the next morning in order to save the ligaments and to save the use of my hand. It was that serious.

Next morning I had the operation and they done a brilliant job and I was due to stay in for five days. That afternoon Ian, Stuart, Jock and the rest of the troops came in to visit me. I felt a bit better seeing all their ugly mugs. I felt even better when I heard that Pascalle and Dell-boy had had some stitches as well. We'd been in a battle and been through a war. Three hours after the op I discharged myself. The op had all been done under a local anaesthetic and I was sitting up watching them. I had 27 stitches. I told them I had to leave, that I couldn't stay there. Fulham old bill came in the night it happened and they tried to question me but I was drowsy and I didn't want to listen to them anyway. They left because I think they thought I'd be in longer and that they'd catch me some other time. The hospital told me if I could sleep for 2 hours and recover a bit then they would give me some tablets and they'd allow me reluctantly to leave for home.

The boys picked me up and we got the one o'clock in the morning ferry back to Dover. I did eat and had a puff but I didn't drink. I just felt relieved that I was on my way home. The boys had heard in the ground that I'd been done badly. When a lot of ours had left us and gone into the ground we'd run the P.S.G. mob twice, and lots of ours thought that was it, the fighting was over. They couldn't believe that it had carried on for well over an hour after they'd left. All in all I rated P.S.G. The stories about them having a top firm was true. I got home to find that my daughters had been in a bit of a panic about what had happened to me. They were just relieved that I was back.

For a few days I just relaxed and chilled out and it even went through my mind not to go to football ever again, and then my mind switched to revenge. But I had to wait a long time, nearly 3 months in all, and in that time I couldn't work. My hand was fucked.

On the day that we had P.S.G. in the return leg at 'The Bridge', we met at a pub near Waterloo Station. It's the pub where Millwall normally wait for Pompey to come into town. We had a top firm there and by one o'clock we was on the move and looking for their firm. Any French we found we terrorized. We then headed for the West End where we heard they was drinking. We found them but couldn't get near them because of the old bill. They had two Brummies with them who we caught hold of and bashed the granny out of. We arrived in a fleet of taxis but the old bill sussed what we were up to. If we had of got hold of them we would have mullered them. They'd turned up 200 handed without tickets, so we knew that in the end the old bill would either take them to the ground or sit tight with them at the pub.

The old bill were being a bit heavy handed and split our mob up so a few of us walked to Piccadilly tube station. As we were going through the barriers a firm of geezers were coming the other way. One of the boys chinned one of them and five of us have gone into about 15 of them. There were cameras everywhere but we didn't care. It was too good an opportunity to iron these cunts out. I steamed in and one of them caught me with a half decent shot and put me down. I was up straight away and chinned him and he went down and never got up. I had five of them around me and backed them off.

The old bill turned up and closed the station it was 5.45 in the evening and rush hour and the Piccadilly Line was closed down because of us. We escaped the coppers and jumped on a train waiting on the platform and Dave and Canning Town were just behind us but both were grabbed by the old bill. Me and Ian were sitting on the train making out this whole thing was nothing to do with us when a woman passenger got off the train and went and grassed us up to the old bill so we were pulled off and had Section 60s put on us. We were searched and taken upstairs and told to sit in a corridor and wait. As we sat there not knowing, what fate awaited us the French came into the station singing and chanting but as soon as they saw us, they shut up. Once they'd gone through, we were put the empty train behind them, which went straight through to Earls Court non- stop.

Before and after the game nothing really happened. We backed them off on the forecourt but it was alive with old bill. I went back to Piccadilly station a few days after the game and spoke to the geezer who was on duty that night and he told me he'd told the old Bill that we didn't start the bother and that we were only protecting ourselves. He told me the police had taken the C.C.T.V. footage away with them but I never heard another thing about it.

My hand slowly healed up but when it's cold in the winter I can feel it and get some pain and discomfort. I can't complain though as it could have been a lot worse. I'd love to go back there again, maybe to play them in the semis or the final of the Champions' League. Now that would be nice.

CHAPTER TWELVE

"JUST SAY NO"

Six months after the events in Paris I had a massive heart attack. A lot of it was to do with what went on in Paris. The shock, the trauma, the being unable to work because of my hand. It was a whole combination of things. In that period, I nearly lost my job because it was impossible for me to work. I'd worked for the same company for years as an asphalter but you need the use of your hands and I couldn't even hold a trowel or the rest of the tools of my trade. In laymen's terms, I was fucked. They were good to me about my injury but they couldn't hold my job open for me indefinitely. Gary, the governor, was even bunging me a £100 a week. You wouldn't get many governors do that for ya?

After the return leg against P.S.G. at 'The Bridge', I sort of perked up a bit. I'd got a bit of revenge and a bit of pride back in my heart after our scuffle at Piccadilly. I was also bang on the old marching powder, not so much in my everyday life but at football, and like a lot of people, the chang played a big part in going to football. A couple of nights a week I'd go out with a few pals and have a serious session on the old Luca Vialli and the booze.

One weekend I was at relaxing home, watching football on the telly. The day before I'd had a Headhunter tattoo done on my lower back and had the crack with Lo Harding who's my mate, and the tattooist. He's done a few tattoos for me and I rate him highly. I went home and had a drink and a Chinese takeaway with me mate Tony from Canning Town.

We did a couple of grams in the afternoon but nothing too serious or heavy. The football came on and Tony phoned and asked how the tattoo was. I was nice and relaxed as we chatted and laughed and then I got a little niggling pain in my chest. I thought it could be indigestion from the previous night's takeaway. To ease the discomfort I took a load of painkillers, drunk a bottle of fizzy lemonade thinking it was maybe wind, and that I needed to burp and move it. About 4 o'clock the pain eased off but what I didn't know or realize was that I'd just had a mild heart attack. If I had gone to the hospital when I had had the first bout of pain then I wouldn't have had what happened next, but because of my ignorance more pain followed. I'm thinking the Anadin and the lemonade have done their job and that I'm now ok. For a good two hours, I was alright, as the pain had gone and I was comfortable.

About 7 o'clock a pain hit me in the chest and I aint kidding it was that sharp it threw me back in the chair. My mouth filled up with saliva, my teeth clenched together, and I hurt like fuck. "What the fucks happening here?" I'm thinking. I was in agony and my mind was in a whirl. I had a funeral to go to the next day and there was no way I was going to miss that. Big Jim, my friend's dad, had some Irish Guards coming to his funeral and I'd been asked to do the job of showing them around and looking after them. To ease the pain I went and laid in a hot bath. I thought the heat might help and if I did get carted off to hospital, I'd be clean. Funny the things you think of at the funniest of times aint it?

I had my bath but the pain persisted so I ended up pacing up and down the room. I must have walked miles and nearly wore the pattern off of the carpet. I didn't know what do do with myself. I never even thought about calling my doctor. My thoughts were if I could get rid of this pain and I could get to sleep then I'd be all right for the funeral the next day. In the end, the pain just got so bad I phoned my daughter and told her that I thought that I was maybe having a heart attack. She asked me to describe the symptoms I was having and I told her my teeth were aching, that I had a pain in my chest and my mouth was filling up with saliva. She asked me if I had any pains in my upper arms, and as she said that, a pain shot up my arm. I told her what had just happened and told her to come over straight away. Now I was panicking. She was only 5 miles away from me so her and her boyfriend Matty was with me in no time. Before they got to me, I phoned for an ambulance and told the operator that I thought I was in the middle of a heart attack I told her my daughter was on her way over. The girl on the other end of the phone told me the ambulance would take about 20 minutes to get to me and if I could get there quicker with my daughter then to come in with her as the ambulance may turn up too late for me. Now I knew I was in serious shit. I jumped in with my daughter as soon as she arrived and as we pulled away from the house, the ambulance turned up and followed us to the hospital.

When I walked into the hospital, I was seen straight away. People were running around all around me as I was laid on a bed. My clothes were cut off me and all sorts of drips put into me. I was really scared and I thought this was me lot, but the hospital staff were brilliant. They couldn't do enough for me. I remember an African doctor coming in and holding my hand and then it hit me that maybe he thought I was dying. "You're all right," he said as her stroked my hand but I could tell by his eyes that he was lying I knew there was something badly wrong. I just wanted to live. I could hear my daughter outside the room crying and that wasn't very nice to hear.

Eventually I was moved onto a ward and when they lifted me off of the bed I'd been lying on, my new tattoo had printed itself into the white sheet where I'd been rolling around in agony. The blood and the sweat had imprinted it into the bed sheets. The skull and cross bones and the wording had come out perfectly. When the drugs kicked in the pain went and only then could I relax. My God, I've never felt pain like it.

The next day I had 45 visitors to see me. I had people from all over the country come and see me. I even had to phone Denton and a few of the Arsenal boys to stop them from coming up. The last thing I wanted was a war in the ward. That would go down well wouldn't it? I'm laying in me hospital bed nearly dying, with me fruit bowl full up and bunches of grapes everywhere and there's a full scale riot going on as 'The Head-Hunters' and The 'Herd' clash at the foot of my bed. Denton's a good pal of mine so I wouldn't put him in any shit. Still, I was glad of the company and I appreciated all those people coming up to see me. It gave me a lift to think so many people cared.

The Chelsea firm was brilliant and everyone rallied round. I stayed in hospital for nine days, was pumped with drugs, and had all sorts of tests. My blood pressure was high, caused by, they said, the regular use of cocaine. One of the doctors told me that a regular user of cocaine will find their blood is four times thicker than someone who doesn't use it and that your heart has to work that much harder to pump the thickened blood around your body. I came clean with the doctor, when I was first admitted, that I'd taken cocaine that weekend and that I was a regular user. They didn't seem shocked. They'd seen and heard it many times before.

On my ward there was a few young faces that had had strokes or heart attacks bought on by the use of Charlie. Drug abuse in this country is rife. If it's not cocaine then it's heroin or pills. Es do ya liver and ya kidneys. Heroin just kills ya.

After ten days, I was allowed out for the weekend and then I was transferred to the London Heart Hospital where I had an operation. My mate Chris from Kilburn worked in there and he was brilliant. He really put me at my ease and looked after me big time. He was there before I went down for my op and he was there when I got back up onto the ward. The operation was frightening. I was cut near my groin and a camera inserted, and they feed it through your body and up to your heart. A stent is placed in your old artery to open it up. The whole process is relayed to a screen above you, beamed back by the camera you have inside you. At one stage I felt a bit queasy and had to look away. Up until then I'd been encouraged by the surgeons to watch the operation. The whole thing took about 45 minutes and it was a strange feeling. You're given a liquid first to drink, which helps the camera to go through your body. You can't feel the camera moving through your body but watching it on the screen is a strange sensation. Afterwards your chest area is very tender and sore.

The operation was a success and I was kept in for three days, and I felt drained both physically and mentally. I'd had a bad year with the stabbing and now the op. I was very low. I was told that to recover fully I needed to stop smoking, to change my diet, and to exercise. It's very hard to do all these things though if you don't have any money in your pocket. To live your life how they want you to live it is hard. I had no job by this time, no income and no money. All I could do was rest.

For a year after the operation, I wasn't allowed to fly so a holiday abroad was out of the question. The next football match I went to was Chelsea v Anderlecht in the Champions League. Chelsea met up at ten o'clock in the morning at Covent Garden. In the away leg I didn't bother going because I knew how it would be. By all accounts, it went mental, and Hicky took the boys on one of his infamous tours.

Cocaine in football and in society in general is rife and it would be nice for everyone to be able to do without it. It's a disgusting habit that's a killer, I think people are unaware of what it really does and can do. People cannot see the dangers. The more you take, the deeper in you get. It's a selfish drug that just takes over you in a feel good way. Since I've stopped taking it I've realized just how boring it really is, and more to the point, how boring the people are who take it. People on it just talk boring cack. I hate it but at one time, I did like it. No, I loved it. Now I wouldn't give you two bob for it. It's disgusting. You wouldn't eat your meals off of a toilet seat but you'd bend down in a public loo, and kneel down, in pools of piss and bits of toilet paper and snort a line off of the carsey. It's total madness. It's filth. Your nose runs, you sneeze, snort and sniff with the effects of the Colombian flu, your eyes bulge and at the time, you think you're clever. Cocaine has taken over the planet and that's sad.

Looking back, I'm glad I had my heart attack. It was a result. It stopped my association with that shit. I've learnt a lesson. I now do things instead of talking about it. I can get on with my life with a clear head. On coke you do a lot of talking and it's mostly talking bollocks. It's a vicious circle of cocaine, cocaine and more cocaine. It's over priced, cut to fuck with all sorts of other gear and overrated. All you're doing is paying money to shorten your life. I swear I will never touch that crap again. I've had the warning, I've had the pain and personally, I now hate it, and hate it with a passion.

So many people now take it at football and it saddens me. I don't preach to people and I don't want to sound like a born again hooligan or Cliff Richard with a Stone Island jacket and a bible, but it's so widespread. I don't think the old bill realize just how readily available it is, not just at football but on the streets. It also makes a lot of people paranoid and over the years at Chelsea, it's caused a lot of in fighting. People are selling gear that is cut to fuck and for your 50 quid you aint getting that much actual cocaine in your gram. Teething powder or talcum powder yes, but real cocaine, no. It's the same if I was selling bootleg booze and I sold you a bottle of vodka that had been half watered down. You wouldn't be best pleased. So why fork out for something that aint the real Macoy? I've heard of glucose, baking powder and even rat poison being used to cut Charlie up with. I've heard some crooks use hay fever tablets and the people using it have said what good gear! All because their noses don't run. Of course, their noses aint going to run if it's cut with fucking hay fever tablets. How fucking stupid are some people? No, it's an evil, evil drug and its fucked loads of firms up, and I hope mobs up and down the country realize one day what it's doing to them and their pals. I really, really hope so. Try it, live without it and you will soon see the difference. Have a spliff and a glass or two of red wine; you'll be far healthier.

CHAPTER THIRTEEN

"COME STAI"

I've always been a big fan of Italian football and especially Napoli because my family originally came from Naples. I've always followed the teams' results and have always followed them closely. They were never the most successful team in Italy as they were always overshadowed by AC. Milan, Inter and Juventus, the big three Northern Italian teams. That all changed when the club signed the little stocky Argentinean, Diego Maradona from Spanish giants, Barcelona.

Maradona made his name with Bocca Juniors before moving to Spain where he stayed from '82 to '84, before moving to Napoli. At Napoli he helped the club win their first Scudetto (title) in 86/87 and again in 89/90. We also lifted the UEFA Cup in the 88/89 seasons. In all he played 259 games for Napoli and scored 115 goals. He was a genius. However, he is best remembered for his "hand of God" goal against England in the quarterfinals of the 1986 World Cup. That's more often talked about than his magnificent second solo goal in the same game. He played in four World Cups in 82/86 and 90/94 and his career spanned nearly two decades. Not bad for a boy born in 1960 in Villa Fiorito, a slum just outside Buenos Aires. He left Napoli in 1991 and returned to Spain, where he played for Sevilla. He was suspended in 1991 from football for 15 months for using cocaine and again in 1994. He once owed over 30 million Euros in tax in Italy.

He had a heart attack in 2004 and bloated up like a pig before having his stomach stapled in a bid to fight the flab. He then went on to to host his own late night T.V. show in Argentina called La Noche del diez (the night of the number 10). Besides all that, he was my favourite footballer of all time. Love him or hate him he was one of the all time greats. It was a big mystery how Napoli could afford to buy Maradona and pay his huge salary and how they even tempted him to join them. They weren't one of the most fashionable clubs in Italy. It was brilliant when he went there and my one regret was I never saw him playing live for them.

The first time I saw Napoli play was in 1994 in a game at Highbury in the Makita Four Team Tournament. Napoli beat Chelsea 2-0, I took my two daughters along, and they loved it. My eldest loves and understands her Italian roots. Napoli had about 30 supporters with them in the West Stand lower. I chatted with the Italians and we had a great bit of banter.

I've visited Italy many times and I've been to Venice, Rimini, Milan and Jesolo, and I've always felt at home. But when I finally got around to visiting Naples I knew I was home. I was meant to go and visit friends and go to a game just before I had my heart attack. I was in touch with the Napoli hooligans or Ultras as they're called out there, through a Chelsea mate of mine who has links with Italian side, Lazio. He deals in a lot of merchandise with them like tee shirts and baseball caps. He also does a lot of the Chelsea Head-Hunter stuff. He put me in contact with one of the leaders or bosses as they're called out there. Dario is one of their main men in their end, the Curva A. Their mob totals about 600-700 in Curva A. The way it works out there is you have the young bosses and then one big boss that runs the show. You also have firms in other parts of the stadium and along with Curva A you also have the Curva B, the Vechhi Lions, the Mastiffs and a couple of other firms within the ground. We've been accepted into the Curva A boys now so I couldn't go anywhere else in the ground. They sometimes fight with one another and they fight with the old bill and in fact, the old bill aren't allowed by the fans into the ground. Imagine that happening here?

I first wrote to Dario and then spoke to him on the phone. He speaks broken English but his English is still better than my Italian. Since them heady days of Maradona and Championship titles, Napoli has had a bit of a fall from grace. Last year they were in the Third Division Serie C, but last season got promotion back to Serie B. This season we play the likes of Juventus who've just been demoted to Serie B, so it should be a good year. Even in Serie C there was violence at the games and the Napoli Ultras are renowned for their toughness and violence. For somewhere like Rome for a game, they'd take twenty thousand supporters. They'd also take maybe ten thousand to watch them play Juventus in Turin.

Naples is a very poor area with loads of unemployment but the fans are fanatical about their team. They'd rather watch football than eat; it's as simple as that. Football comes before anything. They're more fanatical than Newcastle or Sunderland but have a bigger firm than, say, Man Utd. They're more violent and more organized towards violence. Before a game, they meet up early and they don't do chang or drink a lot.

When I did arrange to go to a game out there I first spoke to Dario on the phone, booked my flight and a hotel, and flew out to Napoli the day before the game, with me mate Cooper. When we landed, our mobiles wouldn't work so we had no way of contacting Dario. We gave ourselves a tour of the ground, as the gates were unlocked so we walked straight in, sat in the stands and had a puff. The ground's fantastic and is just outside the city centre. There's a beach nearby which isn't very nice, but just further along the coast is Sorrento where there's some fantastic beaches. There's a big port and it's busy with shipping. We stayed in a little village just outside Naples and it was the bollocks. People were out eating and drinking, it was sunny and locals looked like they were having fun.

The night before the game we got in touch with Dario and they arranged to meet us at midday outside the ground. Me and Cooper, were up early and went over to the ground and although the game wasn't due to kick off for hours there were already fans milling around outside the stadium. There were big mobs of geezers sitting around chatting but hardly anyone was drinking alcohol. It looked like most people were happy drinking little cups of espresso coffee. We had a good walk around, unaware of the time. My mobile went and it was Dario informing me we were 10 minutes late and that we should hurry up. Ten minutes late and they're on the dog and bone. At Chelsea, we get geezers turning up two hours late and no one gives a fuck. Punctuality aint our strong point! "What the fucks up with him?" I asked Cooper. We were just strolling along taking in the atmosphere. We loved it and we even spotted a bloke with a Chelsea shirt on. He was English but he lived in Italy. I spoke to him in the ground but he was a bit of a veg. The Italians wouldn't let him mix with us because they said he wasn't a Head-Hunter. It's the Head-Hunters the Italians wanted to mix with. They like the thought of socializing with the elite of British hooligans. Having a name like

Gaetano Buglioni helps but it would have helped even more if my Italian was a lot better!

The meet when we got there was massive and we soon realized the arranged fight was with the local old bill, and not today's away fans. When we got there the mobs numbers was in the six hundreds. It was a firm and a half. As we walked up to, the leaders of Curva A all eyes were on us and we felt so important. We were like visiting royalty and a guard of honour had come to meet us. It was like being an exhibit in a museum. They were almost star struck. They virtually spunked in their pants looking at us. They loved us. They don't really drink before a game so they didn't want to go out on the piss with us. They have a fight before the game and after the game and if there are no visiting fans then they'll have it with the old bill. Lazio or Roma or Juventus might go there but they'd get smashed.

We were asked millions of questions by all sorts of people about me, English hooligans and the Head-Hunters. I had to swear an allegiance that I've never had anything to do with Lazio's mob. Napoli's main mob at one time were the Blue Lions but they dropped the Blue because they thought there was a strong link between Chelsea and Lazio. There's more West Ham follow Lazio than Chelsea because of the Di-Canio link. I've always supported Napoli and always swore by them. Cooper's now the same and he wears his metal Napoli badge with pride although he won't have a Napoli Tattoo like me.

We were accepted by the Curva A boys and as I say, they swarmed all over us like we were from another planet. Come to think of it, Cooper does remind me a bit like E.T! They bought us drinks and offered us Charlie and the smiles on their faces said it all. They might have changed if we'd turned out to be two black geezers. After all, they'd never seen a photo of me. How would they have welcomed

Lee-Roy and a Winston? I gave away some Head-Hunter pin badges and they gave us caps, badges and tee shirts, which was good. We explained we never had a ticket to get into the game but they told us that we didn't need one. We'd come down the night before to buy tickets when we let ourselves in the ground and the bloke in the ticket office wanted our passports because we were English He explained that it was bad inside the stadium and once inside we were on our own.

There's no police inside the stadium, as the crowd won't let them in. Most of their firm carry blades or wrap belts around their fists so if they had of decided they didn't like the look of us and turned on us we were fucked. "Don't worry," said the bosses, you stay with us, and we walked towards the entrance to part of the stadium, in front of us were lines of old bill. I found out that hardly any of the Curva A boys pay to get in. "Bully, Bully you stay with us," they said and they pointed for me to stay in the middle of the firm. All of a sudden, sticks and lumps of wood were pulled and a battle started with the coppers. We forced our way through into the ground with the old bill defeated. There were casualties on both sides but once inside it still wasn't over.

The ground was packed with fifty six thousand fans and that was for a Third Division game. Part of the ground remained empty though as the Curve B lads in another section, boycotted the game out of principal because of Napoli's demotion from the season before. This was due to financial irregularities. The old bill returned and tried to get into the game and the Curva A lads regrouped and attacked them. It was running battles with the old bill as the coppers, tried to come through some big iron gates. I've run forward and drop kicked the door shut. It sounded like a bomb going off, as it slammed shut forcing the old bill to take a step back. The rest of the lads pushed through behind me and we had the coppers on their toes. Job done. Flares were being fired into the ranks of police but as they were running away, they were stopping and throwing them back towards the chasing Napoli firm. It was an unbelievable sight to see. It was almost surreal.

One of the lads handed me a Napoli scarf to tie around my face in case the police recognized me. I refused it, and told them I was fine without one. Now I was buzzing, as we were victorious. There was plenty of handshakes and backslapping. I was cuddled like a conquering hero. I was now accepted. I'd done my bit. Cooper and me were handed two ice-cold beers and we needed them after all that thirsty work. Someone was dispatched to get the beers and the bloke jumped over the fence, went outside and came back with the beers. The bottles of Heineken went down well. I was offered more Charlie but declined it. Then a big bag of puff was handed to me and when I offered to pay, I was told it came free of charge, as I was a special guest.

In the mob, you have about eight bosses and above them is one big boss. I met the big boss who did his bit by throwing a firecracker into the middle of what visiting supporters there was. It was a good shot too. There were about 500 away supporters and it surprised them. They were covered in by netting above them and wire mesh at the front and sides. They were more or less caged in. The big boss came in with his wife who was a right fucking Pamela Anderson dolly bird look a like. It all goes quiet as all eyes are on him. It's all very dramatic and typical Italian. He didn't have the camel hair overcoat hanging from his shoulders and a baby's leg sized cigar hanging from his lips, but he did have the dark glasses on. He looked very Mafioso. The big boss was aged about fifty-five and he did look the part. He was a big lump that looked game. The club let all this go on and to tell you the truth they can't do a lot about it. If they do try to stop the Ultras then the club would be fucked, the fans run the club. I've never seen so many missiles thrown during a game. The visiting fans and the police are showered with gear non-stop.

When it comes to the actual football its utter shit. It's like watching a conference league side. It's proper cack. This game ended in a 1-1 draw, which saw Napoli go up as champions, very different from the days of Diego Maradona and Chelsea legend and former Napoli favourite, Gan-Franco Zola. Going up, as champions didn't mean a lot to the crowd. There was no wild celebrations or fireworks, it was very subdued. The big boss shook our hands and disappeared before passing his joint to me. I didn't know what to do with it, smoke it or frame it?

After the game only four of the boys came out for a meal with us as everybody heads for home. Apparently no one hangs about after the game It's the Italian way and everybody goes back to their families once the game 'as finished.

At Napoli central, station the queues for the trains were a mile long but the fellas we were with walked straight to the front and no one said a word. The rest of the supporters knew who our escorts were and they were given total respect I've never experienced an atmosphere like it; the smoke, the crackers, the bombs. They even catapult each other into the away supporters end and cut the netting with knives.

We ended up drinking in a little village about three miles outside of Napoli where the actress Sophia Loren comes from. There we met a few of the far right Mussolini supporters who gave us little gifts and bombarded us with a thousand more questions I didn't see one black geezer or Asian in the whole of their firm. They were all Neapolitans and proud of it.

When we drove from the airport towards Naples you can see near on the whole of the city and parts of it looked like a third world shanty town. The food was incredible and the hospitality second to none. It's an experience I shall never forget and I'll be back in the very near future to visit all my new friends. The place, the food, the wine. Well, what can I say? They're my kinda people.

CHAPTER FOURTEEN

THE CHELSEA YOUTH

I first started running with the Chelsea firm in the late 70s. In them days, we were the Shed Boys and we were the firm. Later came The North Stand Boys and then the West Stand and The Benches and then the Gate 13 Boys, who sat in the Lower East Stand and last but not least were the most famous of the infamous. The Chelsea Head-Hunters.

The Headhunters were known worldwide and we were one of the leading brands in hooliganism. A lot 'as been written about the Head-Hunters in the tabloid press and in numerous books, most of it crap and most of it way off the mark, and most of it guesswork. The Head-Hunters were never a sinister right wing organization that had their own bank accounts and rented out muscle to other firms. It just never happened. How could we be far right when we had black geezers in the firm? The colour of someone's skin never came into it and the name Head-Hunters was made up as a bit of a piss take, courtesy of Mr. Hickmott.

In the 80s, it was fashionable for the tabloids to give football clubs' troublesome fans a nickname or a tag. Some firms even named themselves. You had the I.C.F. (The Inter City Firm) the 657 (The Pompey Crew), The Leeds Service Crew. Notice the train theme? Bit too much anorak going on here for me. Anyway, we were the Head-Hunters and I'd say at one stage we were more famous and bigger than the Beatles and there wasn't a choo choo in sight!

In the early 70s Chelsea's firm was mostly made up of youngsters with a smattering of older guys that run the show. The main players were Babs, Hickey, who came along a bit later, Eccles, And God bless him, good old Kojack, Greenaway and The Webbs. The thing with our boys was we had such a big mob. We were split into smaller groups and sometimes there were divisions within the firm. The age group ranged from 13 up to 50 but the majority of the firm as I say was youngsters.

In them days, the youngsters were not known as The Youth or the Chelsea Youth. So where 'as this youth tag came from? Not just with Chelsea youngsters, but clubs from all over the country now have a youth firm. Nowadays you'll hear someone say our youth are having it with so and so's youth. Why youth on youth? Why not just one firm rowing with another? Why does age come into it? I remember Chelsea having a youth movement eight or nine years ago. We had the tattoos done with the skull and crossbones and all the Head-hunter thing and they had "Chelsea youth – never run" but the "never run" was written in German. Don't ask me why.

A few Years back I got chatting to a few of them at Cathy's party.

Years ago, Cathy was one of only a handful of girls that used to run with the firm in the early days, anyway at this do of Cathy's the youth said to me that they needed some help coming through and wanted to get their movement going and to be accepted by the older lads. I gave them a lot of help and a few of them look up to me, and now I think they're the bollocks. They now have their own identity and have a nice tight firm who, if they collar anyone, are like a pack of wolves. They've done their apprenticeship.

I saw them first-hand in Paris and believe me they are good. They took a lot of flack for what happened out in Belgium when we played Anderlecht, but you couldn't blame them. There were a lot of our older lads that went missing that night and I'm sorry to say that night was the same old Chelsea. A big mob, half get restless so a hundred of our lot end up taking on about 500 Anderlecht armed to the teeth. The finger of blame was pointed at the youth but that was so unfair. Our older lot have got to understand and accept that the youth are the future. I don't know if they'll go as long as the Shed Boys or the Head-Hunters, but who knows?

When they are mobbed up, they can pull a firm of 60 to 80 and as I say, they're game fuckers and from what I've seen and heard they must be the top youth firm in the country. They've been in a few scrapes the last few seasons. They done Palace's firm at Wimbledon before a game at The Bridge, and they done Arsenal's main firm at Sloane Square after one Arsenal big mouth called it on with our young lot.

For this Arsenal game we had a big mob in The Adelaide pub on the King's Road and this gobby Gooner phones up and tells us Arsenal are drinking in Sloane Square and spills out all the usual shit about "we're on your manor." How the fuck is Sloane Square our manor?

Sloane Square is for shoppers and out of work thespians that sit outside expensive coffee shops smoking strong French cigarettes with little minge licker dogs on their laps. It's not the HQ of the Chelsea Head-Hunters or the Chelsea Youth. Anyway, our young lot have gone up there 30 to 40 handed and smashed Arsenal to pieces.

When the youth get older will they then become "The Middle Age Firm?" The M.A.F., now that does have a nice ring to it. Perhaps the press will pick up on that. You may one day hear the chant in a far off Northern town as the Football 125 Special pulls in and a chant of "M.A.F., M.A.F., M.A.F." echoes around the concourse. Chelsea's 45 to 85 year old firm will roll into town in their wheelchairs and zimmer frames. Gone will be the Stone Island gear, only to be replaced with tee shirts with Perry Como or Frank Sinatra on the front. The most lethal weapon would be a walking stick. Another tee shirt might read "M.A.F. These colours can't run!"

The thing is everything is stacked against the youth nowadays. The police have better intelligence and have more resources to throw at the problem. The courts dish out bigger fines, prison or Banning Orders and they're the things that have fucked a lot of people. Most of our youth are also local boys who come from Fulham, Battersea, Putney, and Morden. In the Shed Boys and the Head-Hunter days the firm came from right across the Home Counties from Slough, Bracknell, Reading, Basingstoke, Tunbridge Wells, Crawley, Mitcham, Redhill. Our support came from all over the South. The youth had a bit of a tear-up last season with Fulham at a pub on the Fulham Road and by all accounts done a few of Fulham's older lot. To tell ya the truth I didn't even know Fulham had a firm. As long as they keep away from the Charlie and keep that side of things under control then I can't see why they won't flourish and stay around for years to come.

Good luck to them. At least they're not roaming the streets getting into trouble.

CHAPTER FIFTEEN

LIFE AFTER NEAR DEATH

After my heart attack and my operation and the thing in Paris I still go to football. Nothing's put me off from going. I pick and choose now which games I go to. Sometimes I'll go in and watch the game and other times I'll just meet up with my pals and have a few drinks, but I still love the buzz. It's more of a social thing now. At one time there'd be anything up to 50 of us coming down to Chelsea from North London.

We played Celtic recently in a pre-season friendly and 30 of us travelled down to the meet at Russell Square. We had a strong mob out that day with no old bill. In the end there was 120 of us with boys from Oxford, Coventry, Birmingham, Glasgow Rangers, Peterborough, Millwall, and Reading. There was a real mixture and to some people present this was more than football. Celtic was drinking in a boozer just around the corner from Kings Cross but they were wrapped up by the old bill. The mobile numbers we'd been given prior to the game were, surprise surprise, switched off. We did get through to one of Celtic's so-called top boys but he informed us that he was at work and that he would nay be coming to da game, so could we please leave him alone. Bless him, top boy my arse. We then moved off to Sloane Square after we got a call saying that Celtic's firm were on the move and was drinking in a pub just around the corner from Sloane Square. We got off at Sloane Square tube and doubled back around the side streets. When we reached the pub it was empty.

After a few drinks and being closely watched and filmed by the old bill, we moved off down the Kings Road. News came through that Celtic's firm had come off at Fulham Broadway and were drinking in a bar near to the station. Before we could get to them The Youth, who'd been drinking nearby and had also heard where Celtic were, attacked them. They'd burst through the pub doors and got stuck into the Celtic firm, ripping their Irish tri-colour flags and I.R.A. flags down from the windows and the walls. The attack took the old bill by surprise but they quickly restored order and surrounded the pub. No-one went in, no-one came out. This Celtic firm had come 300 miles for a row and then switched their phones off and drank near the ground. Where's the sense in that? They must have bought a one day travel card before they landed at Fulham Broadway. We had heard reports of them being at Westminster Abbey, the Houses of Parliament, Buckingham Palace, Madam Tussauds. What was they on, a fucking guided tour? They knew where we'd be waiting, they knew two days before, but for some reason they just didn't fancy it. Perhaps they're all right giving it the large one to the likes of Stenhousemuir or Falkirk or Alloa, but coming to London and mixing it with the big boys, now that's a different story.

The turn out down at the ground was the bollocks It was just unbelievable. We had a massive mob out on the street waiting for the old bill to escort the Celtic mob down to the ground. Whoever arranged this fixture can't know their football or understand the politics of such a fixture. A couple of times the old bill tried to clear the streets so that they could get the Celtic fans under escort to the ground. Every time they cleared a path then the road would fill back up again. One copper told me to piss off home. "You're not interested in the game," he sneered. "What am I doing here then?" I replied, pulling out a ticket for the game and waving it in his face.

We ended up drinking in the 'La Reserve' bar right next door to the ground and waited for the Jocks to come along.

The game kicked off at 7.45 p.m. and at about 7.30 p.m. the old bill began to move the Celtic firm out of the pub. Again they cleared a way for the escort to proceed and again the road filled back up with fans ready to attack the Celtic escort. Police on horseback were bought in and the same thing happened. They'd clear a path through and instantly the road would fill back up. This Chelsea firm was not going to be bullied out of the way. They were determined to let this Celtic mob know they were there. Eventually the police with horses and dogs forced everyone sideways and backwards and the Celtic fans were marched through at funeral procession pace. Under a hail of abuse they reached the ground just after half time so it took them to walk from Fulham Broadway to Stamford Bridge over an hour. And anyone that knows that distance will tell you it's a two-minute walk under normal circumstances.

Celtic had a mob of about 150 and what a rag tag bunch of scruffy bastards they were. They had all sorts, punks, hippies and students, and donkey jackets seem to be in vogue in their part of Glasgow.

After the game the police held them in for an hour but the Celtic escort still came under attack once they were back out onto the Fulham Road. They came back past the 'La Reserve' and came under attack from a shower of beer bottles.

I like to think that my days at the front of the mob are coming to a close. I'm now 49 but if I didn't go to football I'd be sitting at home twiddling my thumbs. As I say, I pick my games now but you never know, I could turn out to play the old enemy, West Ham or a good F.A. Cup draw could tempt me out, or a Champions League game in Italy. Now we're talking. I was asked by a copper if I was looking forward to the World Cup in Germany but England games don't bother me. I'm Chelsea and I'll fight for Chelsea. I've got a few trips planned this year to go to Naples and hopefully I'll take in 4 or 5 games this season. I'm still not back full time at work, I just do the odd day here and there, roofing. My children are well and they're 21 and 18 and they've both got fellas so they're happy, which means I'm happy. As to where I see myself going from here I really don't know. Maybe one day Italy or even Cyprus, but one things for sure. If I move out to Italy then I'd have to learn the language. With a name like mine I really should speak the lingo fluently. Hello, thank you and fuck off doesn't get you very far out there! The people are great and the language lovely so I owe it to my family to learn it. I've now got time on my hands so who knows?

I don't need a steady woman in my life. I'm all right as I am. I've also now got time to read the many football hooligan books which fill the shelves in most book stores. To be honest some are good and some are downright awful but I aint going to knock anyone. Fair play to them for sitting down and putting pen to paper but the main criteria to writing these books is surely that you have been there and done it and been with the mob at your club. Certain people write these books who have never thrown a punch in their lives What's that all about? Wearing a Stone Island jumper and shaving your head doesn't qualify you as an expert on the scene. It just makes you look a daft cunt.

I liked 'The Governors' by Micky Francis. That was a good read. I think that was one of the first ones. There's been a lot of crap too like 'Amongst the Thugs' and Dougie Brimson and the bullshit he writes. Now that is one sad cunt. Same with the films. It's time a good one came out. 'The Football Factory' weren't too bad but that 'Green Street', was that meant to be serious or what? The accents, the acting, it was just terrible. It was more like a Carry On film. "Carry On Hooligan" it should have been called. No wonder it sunk without trace. Perhaps you'll see Bully on the big screen very soon starring Ray Winstone. Now that would be something!

THE END ... (or is it)

EPILOGUE

It's a crisp sunny November Sunday lunch time and Chelsea are playing Spurs away. A group of 250 Chelsea faces are drinking in a pub near to Pimlico tube station. At 2pm, the pub and the surrounding roads are blocked off by police in full riot gear. For a good half an hour there's a stand off and then eventually one person at a time is allowed to leave the pub, on leaving the pub everyone is asked their name, then photographed and videoed and then searched and then asked to produce a valid ticket for the match. Those without tickets are kept in the pub, those outside are surrounded by police and then after an hour are march to the nearby tube station and are escorted on to a train and after several changes arrive at Seven Sisters underground station. We are then marched along the Tottenham High Road at a snails pace arriving at the stadium 10 minutes before half time. After the game we are surrounded by the police, and are led on a route march around the back streets of North

London, where an hour and fifteen minutes later we arrive at Tottenham hale tube station, only to be met by more police many with dogs. We are then loaded onto a train and after several changes we arrive at Green Park once there we are at last to go our own way. Welcome to the world of the modern football fan, 2006.

We are Chelsea

Scrapbook

CHARITY CELEBRITY
FOOTBALL MATCH
RAISING MONEY
FOR
THE MENINGITIS RESEARCH
FOUNDATION
(REGISTERED CHARITY)

SUNDAY 25th
MAY 1997

VENUE
ENFIELD RANGERS
FOOTBALL GROUND
CARTERHATCH LANE

FEATURING
CELEBRATY ELEVEN
V's
ENFIELD RANGERS SENIORS

KICK OFF
3.30p.m. Approx.
GATES OPEN
2p.m.

£2.00
ADULTS
£1.00
CHILDREN
+O.A.P

EVENING DISCO

£3.00 ADULTS
£2.00 CHILDREN +O.A.P

PRICE INCLUDES
BUFFET, DISCO & CHILDRENS ENTERTAINERS
RAFFLE TICKETS ON SALE AT DISCO

ALL PROCEEDS TO CHARITY
DIG DEEP
TICKET ENTRIES ONLY
THANK YOU

HAVE FUN

GREAT PRIZES

Welcome to our Celebrity XI football match and disco.
As some of you will know, my wife and I decided to organise
this event after our son Luke suffered two attacks of Meningitis.

Meningitis Research Fund was founded by
Steve Dayman our chairman in 1989 following
the death of his fourteen month old son Spencer.
The membership of the Foundation is almost exclusively
people like Steve who have experienced meningitis and
wish to contribute to the battle against the disease.
It is through the marvellous efforts of the Foundation's
members and supporters that our vital work continues.

Meningitis Research Foundation funds a programme of
research into the prevention and treatment of meningitis
at St Mary's Hospital in London and has recently committed
itself to funding 5 new research projects. All the projects
fall within the top 3 priorities of the Foundations research
investment strategy: prevention (vaccine directed research),
improving the speed and accuracy of diagnosis and
developing more effective treatments. The cost funding these
projects is over £1 million spanning three years. The charity
receives no statutory funding and relies entirely upon voluntary
income.

We also run an extensive programme of awareness and public
eduction activities including literature for both the general
public and health professionals, a 24 hour telephone helpline
and other vital information resources. Further information
can be found on the Meningitis research information table
or by phoning our head office in Thornbury on **01454 281811**.

THANKS TO THE FOLLOWING
COMPANIES FOR THEIR GENEROUS SUPPORT

PONTINS HOLIDAYS
SALLY LINE FERRYS
DIXONS GROUP P.L.C.
EARLY LEARNING CENTRE
MARKS & SPENCER P.L.C.
McDONALDS LTD
TOTTENHAM HOTSPUR F.C.
ARSENAL F.C.
M.F.I. LTD
PEARSONS LTD
OTTAKERS BOOKSHOPS
STYLISTIX HAIRDRESSERS
A TO Z STORES (LANCASTER ROAD)
HUNTERS RESTAURANT
SEAN GOODMAN
PRISM LEISURE L.T.D
KINGSTONS BUTCHERS
MAKRO (ENFIELD)
SARACENS
HENRY TILLY LTD
ENFIELD RANGERS FOOTBALL CLUB
AVON
BODY SHOP
BARBER ELLAS
RUTH BROWNLIE
ARNEL LTD

SPECIAL THANK-YOU TO GLAXO WELCOME
FOR THE USE OF THEIR TRADEMARK.

	CELEBRITIES
Manager Dave Barker	Manager Ray Winstone
Asst. Manager Steve Roberts	Ray Winstone - Quadrophenia
	Perry Fenwick - Ellington
Duncan Hunter	Nick Berry - Heartbeat
Brian Francis	Todd Carty - Eastenders
Jason Roberts (Capt)	Steve Harris - Iron Maden
Garth McGirr	Jamie Foreman - Nill By Mouth
Darren Ticehurst	Paul Bully - Stuntman
Conner McGerr	Charlie Creed-Mills - Nill By Mouth
John O'Conner	Gary Webster - Minder
David McCazthy	Leslie Grantham - Paradise Club
Tony Edwards	Phill Danels - Quadophenia
Warren Barker	Terry Marsh -
Lee Draper	Charlie Death - Prime Suspect
Derek Henley	Richard Ercoll - Eastenders
Carlos Smith	John Alford - Londons Burning
Kevin Mackintosh	Mark Robson -
H Coll	Shane Richie -
	Bradley Walsh -
	Brian Conley -

Subject To Commitments

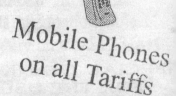

Sewn on to a supporters' flag—the Nazi SS symbol of hate.

Bez gólu (ani z penalty) není vítězství

Sbohem, Evropo!

Celou hodinu hrála Viktoria Žižkov v Jabloneckém cirku proti londýnské Chelsea dobře, promyšleně, systematicky a důsledně rozleptávala dvojnásobnou obrannou linii soupeře, postupně snižovala jeho náskok a kombinacemi hledala cesty ke gólu. Bojovala a ještě před hodinou hry se zdálo, že se blíží k zasloužené odměně — postupu. Krátce poté, co se Viktoria Žižkov dostala až k vedoucí brance, londýnský tým zvýšil bojovnost a důslednost, přidal na ráznosti a během čtyř minut utkání rozfaulovala, ale mnohem lépe než v úterý Slavia.

A v náporu nezastavila. Žižkovské mužstvo prostě udělalo zápas pohledným s přitěžujícím.

Dvoubrankový náskok diktoval Londýnanům taktiku, která Slavii v Praze nedala. Chelsea bránila s devíti hráči ve dvou liniích bystré, koordinované a důsledně už ne daleko středové čáry. A když se dostali do svízelné situace, nerozpakovali se zakopnout míč co nejrychleji do autu.

Trenér Viktory Jiří Kotrba výrazně zamíchal sestavou. Ku prospěchu výkonu mužstva. Jeho důvěru neklamal ani mladíček Michal Šűlhavý (ročník 1976), který bez ligových zkušeností neudělal

v brance chybu. Naopak ve 2. poločase si zkušené poradil s výpadem Wischa. Střídání osou útočníků půl hodiny před koncem, koncepci útočníky neprospělo. Ani mlad. ani Mašek se neprosadil. Tradičně silná zbraň Pražanů — standardní situace — lentokrát k úspěchu nevedla. Ani čtyři volné kopy v dostřelu anglické branky, ani devět rohových kopů, ani a to je nejmrzutější - pokutový kop, který Vrabcovi Charín chytil.

Takže: Sbohem. Evropo! Český fotbal opouští pohárovou scénu proklatě brzo. Po Spartě v PMEZ, Slavii v Viktoria Žižkov i Viktoria Žižkov skončila i Viktoria Žižkov. Oněch 12 bodů, které naše kluby připsaly k našemu evropskému aktivům, je natolik málo, že se pro příští ročníky musíme obávat o pohárová místa. Rozhodně jich nepřibude, spíš hrozí, že v nejprestižnějším PMRZ pro nás místo nezbude. A to by byla rána: sportovní i ekonomická.

VÍT HOLUBEC

Los druhého kola

Pohár UEFA: Hunvři Budapešř - Bayer Leverkusen, Newcastle United - Athletic Bilbao, GKS Katovic - Girondins Bordeaux, Juventus Turín - Maritimo Funchal, 1. FC Kaiserslautern - Odepв BK, Rapid Bukurešť - Eintracht Frankfurt, AC Parma - AIK Stockholm, Admira Wacker Vídeň - AS Caunes, Dynamo Moskva - Real Madrid, Trabzonspor - Aston Vila, Lazio Řím - Trelleborg FF, FC Sion - Olympique Marseille, Slovan Bratislava - Borussia

Dortmund, Tekstilščik Kamyšin - FC Nantes, Wacker Innsbruck - Deportivo La Coruña, Boavista Porto - SSC Neapol.

PVP: FC Porto - Ferencváros Budapešř, FC Bruggy - Panathinaikos Atény, Sampdoria Janov - Grasshoppers Curych, Besiktas Istanbul - AJ Auxerre, Feyenoord Rotterdam - Werder Brémy, Arsenal Londýn - Bröndby Kodaň, Tatran Prešov - Real Zaragoza

Lokvenc na Žižkov

Fotbal - Jednání o přestupu 21letého hradeckého fotbalového útočníka Vratislava Lokvence spěje k svému závěru. Talentovaný hráč by se měl již v příštím týdnu objevit na Viktorii Žižkov. O hráčské náhrade se rozhodne v nejbližších dnech.

Jak v Řecku?

Volejbal - V Řecku pokračovalo MS volejbalistek. Skup A: Rusko-Kanada 3:2, Řecko- Alžírsko 3:0. B: USA - Argentina 3:0, Brazílie - Německo 3:0. C: Čína-Japonsko 3:0, Itálie - Bulharsko 3:0. D: Nizozemsko - Korejská republika 3:1, Kuba - Švédsko 3:0.

Světový rekord

Plavání - Australanka Mary Mainaová vytvořila při MS veteránů plavců ve Světových hrách veteránů v Brisbane neoficiální světový rekord v plavání na 50 metrů volným způsobem v kategorii 160 až 104 let. Padesátimetrovou vzdálenost překonala stylem znak za 5:12,34 min.

Rallye do Izraele

Motorismus - Předposlední dílčovou soutěž letošního kalendáře Mezinárodní automobilové federace je Rallye faraonů, která začíná v neděli 2. října v Alexandrii. Letos poprvé podsedky zavítaji kromě Egypta také do Izraele.

IAAF ratifikovala

Lehká atletika - Mezinárodní atletická federace (IAAF) oficiálně ratifikovala světový rekord amerického sprintera Leroye Burrella v běhu na 100 m, který dosáhl 6. července na mítinku v Lausanne časem 9.85

Novotná dál

Ohlasy britského tisku

Londýnské deníky jásají nad postupem Chelsea v Poháru vítězů po poháru.

Daily Telegraph: **Chelsea si sice nevypracovala žádnou šanci, ale ani ji nepotřebovala, neboť její obrana byla velmi odolná.** "The Guardian: **Nebyl to sice pohledný výkon, ale vitalí na to, aby Chelsea mohla oslavovat.** "Daily Mirror: "Charin předvedl v Jablonci svou vlastní "Bohemian Rhapsody".

Vedl, jak Vrabec kope penalty a chytil mu ji. Nešťastný italský rozhodčí zápas pokazil tím, že používal příliš často píšťalku. "Daily Express: **Vedoucí tým české ligy skončil zápas ve stavu úplné frustrace.**"

■ Policie České republiky měla v Jablonci možnost ukázat své umění při zneškodňování protivníka. Jak se jí to podařilo, posuďte sami.

■ Zneškodněný protivník...

■ Radost přiznivců Chelsea z postupu

Rowdies tentokrát v mezích normy

Na čtvrteční pohárové utkání Chelsey s Viktorií Žižkov přijelo do Jablonce téměř patnáct set anglických fanoušků. Policie měla pohotovost již od středy. Chelsea se snažila jejich příjezd zorganizovat, avšak několik stovek jich přijelo silově. Ještě před utkáním Express vyzýval jednoho z nich. **Dlouho jsme neměli na pohárové zápasy, téměř všichni**

z nás se opravdu chovají slušně. V Jablonci se mi moc líbí, je tu dobré pivo a hezká děvčata. Hlavně však, aby Chelsea postoupila." řekl nám Jeff Brockman z Londýna.

Dlouho před utkáním byla v Jablonci více policistů než auditorů, s kterými až na men-ších rowdies, se kterými si si výjimky zvládli. Před

vstupem na stadion byly nainstalovány detektory, které jen nekolik zadržených ty....

Münchenem, přemlsvil Vik-torky příjelo jen velice málo. Hlavní tribuna au.... stadiónu Hlavního městě Angličanem, kteří se jablonec-kým rowdies chovat ve svem mužstvo.

Kritice před utkáním polície zorganizovala agent Angličanů, kteří se nakonec....

Michal Bílek: „Postup jsme si prohráli už v Londýně"

Nakopávání míčů k ničemu

Po vítězné Viktorie Žižkov z Poháru vítě-

pouštěli. Škoda nejroznáměné penalty, ta

○ V čem vy, jako kapitán a zkušený fotba-

STD CHEAP DAY   RETURN   VALID FROM 31 MARCH 1996

From BIRMINGHAM BR   VALID UNTIL 31 MARCH 1996

To   LONDON BRIT RAIL   Adult ONE   Child NIL

RouteANY PERMITTED

Journey details (for codes see over)   Coach seat N/S Accom.

VALID ON ANY TRAIN

Issued at   1052   70 15001601 02611 28MCH96   10.10   C/CARD £24.00   For conditions see over
OUT   31MCH96 1072   0418   00000   CTR 6TNHXX43

Chelse Youth

"You've been dealt with and left
by Londons Premier Youth firm"

Introducing
The
Elite

CYF

*We don't just win
battles.
We Win Wars.*

ENGLANDS FINEST
YOUTH

replacing him with Garry Chivers.

Chelsea fans were packed into the Goldhams Common end of the ground but there seemed plenty of room in the areas reserved for home supporters even though tickets were on sale at the turnstiles for the League Cup tie against Aston Villa.

The game kicked off early and there was a scare for United before 3 o'clock when Chelsea centre forward Colin Lee got past Lindsay Smith before Steve Fallon came to the rescue.

United hit back quickly with Derrick Christie having a shot blocked before a poor clearance by Droy gave Roger Gibbins a chance to unleash a fierce volley which goalkeeper Peter Borota took high up.

SCUFFLES

Chelsea forced a first corner of the game after four minutes, United replying with one of their own two minutes later after Reilly had got through on the right. Both kicks were easily cleared.

Visiting defender, Dennis Rofe, achieved the distinction of being booked for time wasting with 80 minutes to go.

There were some scuffles at the Newmarket Road end where it looked as though a few Chelsea fans had managed to infiltrate the home supporters.

About a dozen supporters climbed over the barrier on to the pitch to get away from the fighting but the police restored order after a couple of minutes.

Back on the field United were beginning to take just as firm a hold.

Steve Fallon joined the attack after a quarter of an hour and beat Droy in the air to flick on Spriggs' cross to Tom Finney who headed straight at Borota.

Soon after United went close to scoring three times in the space of only two minutes.

Reilly headed wide after a good cross by Evans which Donaldson would have been proud of and, seconds later, a superb through ball by Roger Gibbins sent the lanky Scot racing for goal.

But Borota who seems to play as much outside his area as in it, got there first to clear.

With Chelsea reeling, Derrick Christie cut through on the left and hit a long cross to Spriggs who did well to control the ball at the far post but then slammed it at the post as Borota flung himself forward.

The extrovert Yugoslavian keeper amused the crowd but terrified his defence a few minutes later when he ran five yards out of his area and back heeled the ball to a team mate.

United were running the game, but occasionally leaving themselves alarmingly open at the back where Smith did not look his usual assured self.

After the early trouble the terraces were quiet but 10 minutes before the break a fight broke out in the main stand which resulted

in three Chelsea supporters being ejected and a United steward being led away bleeding from a face wound.

Five minutes later United seemed to have got the goal which their overall play deserved when Gibbins fired home from close range. But as United celebrated the referee was pointing for a free-kick in Chelsea's favour, apparently for handball by Gibbins.

United kept the pressure on as half-time approached and Borota had to pull off a diving save from Reilly before Finney shot over the bar.

Half-time: United 0, Chelsea 0.

Seconds after the re-start the Chelsea defence was reduced to total shambles yet again, but United had to suffer the frustration of having another goal disallowed.

It was Finney's foot which added the final touch as the penalty area was turned into a confused shooting gallery but the flag was up for offside.

Almost immediately Reilly was through on to a Christie pass but wasted a chance with a weak shot straight at the 'keeper.

Chelsea launched an attack after 57 minutes, a rare and unexpected event which ended with a mis-hi

Sports Telegraph

4,643

THE LATE SATURDAY EDITION OF THE Evening Telegraph

PRICE 14p

SATURDAY, MAY 12, 1984.

Crowd spill holds up game

GRIMSBY Town's match was delayed for eight minutes this afternoon as hundreds of Chelsea fans spilled over on to the pitch from the Osmond Stand.

But the police, who were mounting their biggest-ever operation for a football match in Humberside, stressed later it was not a pitch invasion.

"People were in danger of being crushed and, for safety reasons, we allowed a number over the barriers and then escorted them to another part of the ground," said Sup. David Hopwood, who

was directing the police operation.

While the players were off the pitch Chelsea chairman Ken Bates walked out in front of his club's supporters to plead with them to continue to behave themselves.

Some 6,000 tickets had been sold to Chelsea fans but some estimates put the number of the London club's supporters arriving at nearer 10,000.

Most pubs in the area closed their doors to football fans but there was some anger from traders in the Park Street area that the supporters were still able to buy drink from

the supermarket owned by Town director Mr. Ron Ramsden.

But when managing director Mr. Dudley Ramsden was contacted by the Evening Telegraph, he said he wasn't aware of what was happening at the store and immediately instructed his staff to stop selling alcohol and to refuse to admit anymore football fans.

29 victims in night of fear

by Danny Buckland

SOCCER hooligans went on the rampage in a night of violence and destruction in Brighton.

Gangs clashed in battles in the town centre and police made 34 arrests.

Chelsea fans ran riot throughout the night and 29 people ended up in hospital.

Two Londoners, aged 19 and 20, were detained overnight. One of the youths, badly wounded by a Stanley knife, needed an emergency operation.

The sickening catalogue of violence began as more than 300 Chelsea supporters arrived in town for today's match against Albion — the Brighton club's first home game of the season.

"It was evil, the worst trouble I have ever seen," said Mr Derek Baker, landlord of the Carpenters Arms in West Street.

"We tried to keep the fans out but they just swamped us. I had two men on the door but they were just swept aside. The fans kept taking glasses and bottles and went outside to throw them.

"They were rampaging about, kicking and punching each other. It was awful."

A man was severely gashed in the face after a beer glass was smashed into his face at a town centre pub.

At 9.30 p.m. a 21-year-old man was viciously attacked by a gang and needed 22 stitches in his wounds.

In the early hours of the morning a middle-aged man and his wife were attacked in New Road. The man's head was split open after being hit with a dustbin lid.

About 70 police officers in mobile units tried to quell the trouble as the youths ran riot. The police rounded up a 100-strong gang, forcing them into the subway at the bottom of West Street which was turned into a makeshift prison.

Police blocked off one end by locking gates with handcuffs, and dog handlers sealed off the other end.

A group of 60 Londoners were taken under police escort back to the capital

Ambulancemen said they dealt with casualties from fights in New Road, West Street and the Clock Tower. A youth had his face slashed after a row at a chip shop in Ship Street.

England soccer fans on rampage

by GERAINT JONES

HUNDREDS of England soccer hooligans left a trail of destruction early today as they went on the rampage in Norway.

Between 50 and 70 obs were arrested and least one supporter ajured as police used ar gas and batons to ell the violence.

Clashes erupted despite a crackdown in nich Stephen Hickmott was kicked out of orway in handcuffs.

Our exclusive picture ows Hickmott, 37, ao has a string of soccer convictions, leaving slo airport. Police say was the ringleader of army of Swedish fans. Trouble began early

Turn to Page 2

Today EXCLUSIVE

SPITTING MAD

Hooligan Stephen Hickmott in full war cry at one soccer match

Me a soccer thug . . I was only flogging T-shirts

A SOCCER yob was booted back to Britain spitting and kicking yesterday after an anonymous tip-off that he planned to invade Norway.

Norwegian police believe Stephen Hickmott, 37, had become the boss of a violent group of Swedish fans and planned to lead them across the border for a fight during tonight's vital World Cup clash with England.

But the former Chelsea Headhunters soccer gang member, who was deported in handcuffs, says he was in Norway to sell T-shirts.

A senior Norway police source told TODAY: "We are confident he was here to make trouble and we are glad to have removed him in advance."

Hickmott was officially deported for intending to sell souvenir T-shirts for last night's Bruce Springsteen concert without a permit.

Five more fans will follow him today in the clampdown following a joint police operation between Britain, Sweden and Norway.

Hickmott spat, swore and kicked out at journalists as he left Oslo airport for Heathrow, where he was greeted by Special Branch officers.

After his arrival, the crop-haired fan insisted he was innocent.

He said angrily "I have not committed any crime. It is all to do with 200 Bruce Springsteen T-shirts I had wanted to sell.

"It is nothing to do with the match."

But his temper snapped as he stepped off the Scandinavian Airways flight, guarded by three

Hickmott arrives at Heathrow yesterday

by DAVID JONES and RICHARD CREASY

Norwegian police officers. He shouted abuse at photographers as he was bundled to two British officers who escorted him through Terminal 3.

A crowd of 30,000 is expected at England's top-of-the-table match. Only 1,350 tickets have been allocated to the official England Travel Club, but up to 4,000 fans are expected to converge on the Ulleval stadium.

One Englishman was in a serious condition in hospital last night after a fight between fans and doormen in Oslo. The

race to find Hickmott — who has a string of convictions for soccer violence — began after an anonymous letter was sent to police in Sweden three weeks ago.

A spokesman for the National Soccer Intelligence Unit in London — which has supplied information to the Scandinavians on Hickmott — confirmed the contents of the anonymous letter.

Hickmott, from Tunbridge Wells, Kent, has convictions stretching back to 1974.

They include robbery, criminal damage, threatening behaviour, breach of the peace and carrying an offensive weapon.

England fans on rampage

From Page 1

this morning in Oslo after supporters for tonight's England World Cup qualifier against Norway spilled on to the streets as pubs closed.

Scores of extra officers wearing riot shields were drafted in as gangs of thugs roamed the streets, wrecking pubs and restaurants around Oslo's central station.

An Oslo police spokesman said early this morn-

ing: "Although we have contained the area of trouble it shows no sign of stopping.

"Many of our pubs open until 4am which does not help the problem."

An estimated 1,000 fans travelled from England for tonight's match.

The hooligans were first reported to have run amok just after midnight at a pub which had been adopted as an unofficial

headquarters for England supporters. Police had been watching The Pallet and moved in quickly, surrounding it with dogs, batons and riot shields.

Despite their quick action, the pub was reportedly wrecked.

Trouble broke out later at a second pub, the Sir Winston, when English yobs refused to leave.

At least five ringleaders and a dozen injured fans face deportation today.

Riot police stand guard over a huddle of fans outside a smashed Oslo bar

Police put youths behind bars in a seafront subway

Chelsea fans storm pitch

AT the end of today's gam Chelsea fans stormed al over the pitch, broke th crossbar at the North en of the ground and a battl broke out with the police.

This left several people injured on the pitch who were stretchered off.

The violence erupted in other parts of the ground and police were powerless to deal with the disgraceful scenes.

Two of the injured were policemen who had to be taken off by stretchers, one was led off clutching his face while other officers drew truncheons to protect their colleagues.

DETECTIVES uncovered a cache of petrol bombs in Brighton today.

Police sealed off a cul-de-sac just behind Bond Street where a crate full of the crudely-made bombs were found.

It is believed the bombs are connected with an incident during last night's violent scenes involving soccer fans.

29 victims in night of fea
—Page 2

Night of terror hooligans fined

FIVE football hooligans were today fined a total of almost £1,000 for their part in last night's violence.

Magistrates dealt a hefty blow to fans with a firm message that such behaviour would not be tolerated.

Clerical officer Michael Greenway, 38, of Sandhurst Road, London SE6, was fined £300 after pleading guilty to using threatening behaviour.

He was among a group of fans chanting "Chelsea" and making V signs in West Street, Brighton.

Greenway told police officers: "One of the Chelsea fans has got stabbed so we are going out to get them," the court heard.

Peter Didcote, 18, of Freshfield Road, Brighton, was ordered to pay £200 after pleading guilty to acting in a

way likely to cause a breach of the peace.

Insp. Graham George said Didcote swore at police when advised to go home, and he began taunting a group of fans in West Street.

Steven Gillan, 20, of Worlds End, Chelsea, admitted dropping his trousers and revealing his backside in West Street, and was fined £100 for behaviour likely to cause a breach of the peace.

Kicked

Labourer Albert Southern, 18, of Springfield Road, Brighton, claimed he kicked out at someone who had hit his girlfriend in Duke Street Brighton..

He was fined £200 togethe with a further £50 for being i breach of a previous order.

Audio typist Elizabet Cubitt, 23, of Stanhope Roa London NW1, was fined £1

for using threatening words and behaviour in North Street, Brighton.

The fans were among 13 being dealt with by magistrates today. Seven have London addresses.

Ninian arrests

AT least a dozen arrests were made before half time at this afternoon's Cardiff v Chelsea match as violence flared on the terraces and outside Ninian Park.

A major police operation had been mounted in a bid to prevent problems.

Many Chelsea fans climbed from the enclosure into the grandstand, preventing ticket holders from taking their seats. Others climbed over a wall into areas containing City fans, and began chanting their team's name.

City followers retaliated, and police moved in to separate them.

News in brief

17 arrested after Chelsea fans fight rivals in cemetery

RIVAL football fans were arrested as they clashed ahead of Chelsea's friendly against Celtic at Stamford Bridge. Police detained 10 Chelsea supporters and seven Celtic fans for various public disorder offences and minor assaults before yesterday's pre-season game.

There were reports of fighting in West Brompton cemetery and the Met said there had been one assault and three disturbances in the Fulham Road, but there was no trouble during or after the game which ended in a 1-1 draw.